D1101806

Angela Donovan is a world-class psychic detective, spiritual life coach and medium. Her international clients number the rich, the royal and the famous, and she has appeared on TV and in the media in Great Britain, Europe, the USA, Canada and central Asia.

Angela has trained many others to develop their supernatural powers. Now, for the first time, she shares the secrets of her psychic success in this, her phenomenal new book.

THE SECRETS OF PSYCHIC SUCCESS

The Complete Guide to Unlocking Your Psychic Powers

ANGELA DONOVAN

RIDER

LONDON SYDNEY AUCKLAND JOHANNESBURG

1 3 5 7 9 10 8 6 4 2

Copyright © 2007 Angela Donovan

All rights reserved. No part of this publication may be reproduced, stored in a
retrieval system, or transmitted in any form or by any means, electronic,
mechanical, photocopying, recording or otherwise, without the prior permission
of the copyright owner.

Angela Donovan has asserted her right to be identified as the author of this
Work in accordance with the Copyright, Designs and Patents Act 1988.

First published in 2007 by Rider,
an imprint of Ebury Publishing, Random House,
20 Vauxhall Bridge Road, London SW1V 2SA

Random House Australia (Pty) Limited
20 Alfred Street, Milsons Point, Sydney,
New South Wales 2061, Australia

Random House New Zealand Limited
18 Poland Road, Glenfield,
Auckland 10, New Zealand

Random House South Africa (Pty) Limited
Isle of Houghton, Corner Boundary Road & Carse O'Gowrie,
Houghton 2198, South Africa

Random House Publishers India Private Limited
301 World Trade Tower, Hotel Intercontinental Grand Complex,
Barakhamba Lane, New Delhi 110 001, India

The Random House Group Limited Reg. No. 954009

Papers used by Rider are natural, recyclable products made from wood grown
in sustainable forests.

Printed and bound in Great Britain by Mackays of Chatham plc, Kent

A CIP catalogue record for this book is available from the British Library

ISBN 978-1-8460-4059-7

If you have opened this book and are reading this,
then you are ready for the most powerful psychic journey.
Once started, there is no going back.

Contents

Foreword
by Johnnie Walker

With her wonderful mane of golden hair, Angela Donovan was a ray of sunshine when she came into my life several years ago.

Angela had been strongly recommended by those in the know as a highly gifted psychic in whom one could have complete trust. I was feeling pretty low at the time, but after an hour with Angela I left with a new sense of hope and optimism for the future. She was telling me all kinds of amazing things about myself even as she was brewing herbal tea in the kitchen. Angela made the world of spirit – contact with guides and loved ones – seem as natural as picking up the phone and having a chat.

I developed complete trust in Angela over subsequent meetings, safe in the knowledge that our chats would remain totally confidential and that she would never impart any information to me that I wasn't able to deal with.

'It's all within you. I just help to bring it out and be your messenger, guided by those that know.' For one so gifted, her humility is an inspiration.

Aside from visits for readings, Angela and I developed a good and lasting friendship and, when possible, we'd meet up in London to go to her favourite little cafe for egg and chips. (We've done some pretty good restaurants together as well.)

The most amazing thing Angela ever told me was regarding a 'very special woman' who would come into my life at the right moment. 'This woman is quite unlike any you've had relationships with before. She's small, with curly dark hair and she is everything in one fantastic package – very attractive, great personality, wonderful cook, full of fun and laughter and very intelligent. She will be so good for you. I see you side by side on planes. You'll travel a lot together for holidays and for work.'

'She sounds amazing,' I replied. 'When do you think she'll come into my life?'

'Not yet – you're not ready. It will happen at the right time.'

I'd pretty much given up on ever meeting this amazing woman, and it would be another three years before, quite by chance, I finally met Tiggy. Her appearance was exactly as Angela had described, and she had all the qualities, and more, that Angela had mentioned. Tiggy arrived just in time to help and support me through cancer and the subsequent treatment. Without her I'm not sure I'd have made it through my illness. And we have indeed sat side by side on many plane trips, both for holidays and work, to many far-flung destinations, including India, America, Canada and Australia.

In addition to her gifts as a psychic, Angela is a warm, kind-hearted and always well intentioned human being with a boundless love for humanity and for all those in the animal kingdom.

Angela, to really know what I think of you, all you have to do is drop the last 'a' from your name. I thank you for all those occasions when you have given me a much needed lift during the difficult times and for now also giving me the honour of writing the foreword for your book.

So many of us have at times wondered how we ourselves

can get in touch with the intuition and psychic power within. To reveal and set free all the wonderful knowledge and wisdom in the following pages is to offer a true gift to the world.

May the light you have spread come back to you and make you shine ever brighter, for always and ever.

God bless you.

Johnnie Walker, MBE
London, September 2006

Acknowledgements

I give my blessings and love to the souls who sat round a table with me in another dimension, before I came into this physical life, and who contracted to meet up with me here at the times we agreed in order to progress our spiritual journey.

I especially give love and deep gratitude to the one being who said we couldn't meet until later, at a time when we had both experienced enough lessons of learning to finish our journeys together. That is to Andrew, my husband, my best friend, my grounded partner, my confidant in all things material, emotional, physical and spiritual. I also offer him my thanks for sharing some of his immense creative gift by penning the cartoons for this book.

Great smiles and blessings, too, to the lofty beings who hold the truth and are still sharing the knowledge with me, a mere mortal caught up in physical living but who has never forgotten that she's only the messenger.

To Jack, my stepfather, for avidly questioning and disagreeing in true engineering manner, thereby benefiting my work enormously and guiding me gently towards using the pathways of reason and logic within my research.

To Sheena for being who she is, a great being. I recognised her immediately we met, each of us arriving right on time for both to pass on our spiritual message through writing our documentaries and film.

THE SECRETS OF PSYCHIC SUCCESS

To Kasia, my Polish support, for 'sensing' my call and responding positively by coming to live in our hectic home; for her generosity, spirit and humour, and for the gifted way in which she drew the original diagrams for this book.

To all those who have called themselves students of spiritual learning, and especially to Kate, for sticking it out with such determination and for still being there even when I need pulling up mentally for taking her for granted.

And to Tony LeRoy, my spiritual twin in NY, to Susan Mears, my agent who has the 'knowing', and to Sue Lascelles, my gifted editor, and the Team at Rider for knowing all along it was coming!

All of our journeys have only just begun.

Introduction

To see or not to see, that is the question. Or at least one of them. OK, so what will being psychic do for you? Well, truly it will shift your life forwards in ways you can hardly imagine just yet. From the moment you start using this book psychic experiences of the 'strange but true' variety will become regular occurrences. Don't be alarmed, they are all part of the journey, and as we go along I will explain many such apparently inexplicable mysteries to help you on your road to a whole new awareness.

In buying this book you have chosen to open up an immense power lying dormant within you. This power is your fundamental right, even if no one has ever told you about it. Being in the physical body is like living in a house with tightly sealed shutters over all the windows, and it takes effort, and effort takes energy, to open them up and let the light flood in.

Be aware – when you start working with this power you will become a beacon of dynamic, pulsating energy and a highly tuned receiver and transmitter. Psychics can read other people's thought waves – in itself a great gift – but you and I are going to go much further up the mountain and learn to pick up on the energy fields around the living, read the imprints left on inanimate objects and activate your secret antenna to get messages from both the future and beyond the grave. Spooky, isn't it?

But the idea, as I repeat throughout the book, is for you to be in total control at all times and, with the protocols I'll be giving you, you will be. So even though this may be the first time you've succeeded in getting in touch with your own psychic power, you'll enjoy the process.

Are you a positive or a negative type of person? Are you a pessimist or an optimist? Is your glass half empty or half full? Give the question thought right now, as your personal view will have a very great effect on the way you decipher psychic messages and speak what you receive when eventually passing them on to others.

My glass is always full to the brim. From this viewpoint I am going to be taking you through the true values of negativity and positivity. Every living being is surrounded by an energy field via which they instinctively sense others' moods. Indeed, every life form on earth is capable of perceiving our moods and will be affected by them. I am going to show you how to change your moods to create a more positive energy field, while at the same time altering your attitude towards life. You will love yourself and find gratitude for being alive and awakened at this time. Believe me, it is your absolute right to enjoy it all and be happy! You will laugh a lot more too.

But becoming a great psychic is not only about discovering the power you are seeking to awaken; it is also about working with it wisely, positively and correctly on command once you have discovered it. So while later in the book I will be teaching you how to be psychic using your mind alone, in Chapter One I will be giving you some of the tools psychics can employ to access and use their psychism skilfully. There are many such tools to choose from – including cards, tea-leaves, runes and palmistry. Each one is there to complement the psychic's power as they feel suits them best. So if, for example, you are drawn to work with a pendulum when you've finished this course, then by all means do so, and learn how to become the best with that.

The following chapters take you through the different stages of your psychic development, giving you plenty of chances to put the work into practice in rewarding and exciting ways and start achieving genuine, demonstrable results. I would ask you not to rush on to the end, however, no matter how enthusiastic you are (and I'm a fine one to talk!). Take the steps one at a time. Complete each 'wake-up call' (my term for the exercises in this book) thoroughly and successfully before moving on to the next. Once mastered, together they will become a source of enlightenment that will stay with you forever.

This book is unique in its methods and formula. I received it from souls who teach in the spirit dimension. It is thus a divine order of learning which, when followed with intent, will give the student an open doorway to an amazing life. Trust must counteract fear. Joy in the moment must alleviate worry.

When I was first invited to appear on TV, in the nineties, it felt good. I loved the idea and trusted myself to go with the flow. Since then I have shared my keys to 'mind power' with countless people and am constantly delighted at just how many around the world have improved the quality of their everyday lives through learning these psychic skills. They have learnt to be the best, the best for themselves.

By finding your psychic power you will create a magical shift in yourself that will – quite delightfully and gently – open you up to your true consciousness. And in so doing you will be introduced to an incredibly special world, one that nobody ever told you existed – not because you didn't ask but simply because they didn't know!

As a messenger, I wish to share all possible information with you so you can realise this gift and achieve the most meaningful wake-up call of your life. Please know that any effort you take to advance beyond the skills offered in this book will only increase your innermost power and energy; by determining to offer service to others you will find you are offered limitless rewards.

Finally, it is my wish that this book will show you, in easy-to-follow steps, how best to use all of your nascent ability to reconnect with the true soul power you had before beginning this life, and to which you will naturally return on your death and passage to the afterlife.

Enjoy the journey. It's an amazing ride.

With my love, thoughts and smiles,

Angela Donovan

KEEP IT SIMPLE

I love quotes and this one, from Einstein, is my favourite: 'I have a simple mind, so I worked on keeping everything simple and it helped me.' I'll try to do the same here.

WHAT IS A PSYCHIC?

According to the *Collins English Dictionary* a psychic is someone who:

> . . . has strange mental powers which cannot be explained by scientists, such as being able to read the minds of other people or to see into the future, e.g. 'How did you know I was coming?' – 'I must be psychic.' It also means relating to the mind rather than the body.

That's all it says. It doesn't help a lot, does it? The reduction of the term to such a simplistic view tells us little about the subject – and perhaps rather more about the compiler. Being 'psychic' – or 'sensitive' (a term I prefer) – involves far more than having 'strange mental powers which cannot be explained by scientists' or 'being able to read the minds of other people or see into the future', as this book will show you.

Currently, it would seem that the general public understand a psychic to be someone using intuition and the sixth sense only. This is not really surprising. With inadequate definitions like the one above, how can people be expected to know or understand anything more? Perhaps the prevalence of this limited view is also due to the ongoing run of paranormal and psychic shows on UK satellite TV channels in the past few years. If the media has no greater idea of the true depth of this work and what fun it can be, of course that is going to be reflected in the public view. But at least the subject is now reaching a much wider audience, and I'm delighted that such programmes are creating a greater interest in psychism, even if it is not yet the deeper one it warrants.

The term ESP (extra-sensory perception) is often used almost as a synonym for psychic ability, but to me this term denotes being able to receive and decipher communications from elsewhere, i.e. from the higher wavebands, including thought waves. So let me set down what I believe a true psychic is. We will be adding to this definition as we go along.

In essence, a psychic is a person who has, through their conscious will, perfected the ability to tap into frequencies normally beyond the capability of the physical senses. This gives them an open doorway to sounds, vibrations and visions from other dimensions within the Earth's sphere, and in some cases from across the universe. Forget all about time and distance, communication is readily available from people who have long since been dead and buried in the physical sense, as well as from those in different time zones. For the real adept, the power available is truly immense – it's only when such people try to be 'normal' and behave like more ordinary human beings that problems arise.

I also believe that a psychic's hit and miss – success or failure – rate is subject to their levels of perception and training. Can you imagine the effect on humankind if suddenly everyone had instant, total psychic ability all at once? Most couldn't or wouldn't cope. So it stands to reason that overall the development of psychism has to be a gradual process of understanding, spread perhaps over many years or even lives, for the majority of us to get there.

In my experience there are three main ways in which a psychic develops or comes into being.

First, there are those for whom the human body chosen for this life has a part of the brain already activated, not lying dormant as is more usually the case. For these individuals, psychic experiences will start in early childhood and, depending on the child's upbringing, either become enhanced or dulled by orthodox education as they grow up. But the psychic dimension is never completely shut off, so such people are always open to belief and have the potential for a healthy interest in this work.

Second, there are those who experience a severe emotional trauma – I've met several psychics who came into this work after the death of a loved one – or suffer a physical shock, such as a blow to the head. This can literally open up the 'doorway' receiver. This is all well and good if the person seeks to understand what is happening to them, but if not, it can be very disconcerting. A blow to the head, for instance, can cause voices to be heard – somewhat as if the radio has been left on between stations. As the voices are likely to be from the 'lower' levels (more on that later), this may be particularly disturbing. So it is vital for the individual's sanity that they understand what is happening to them and learn how to take proper control.

Third, there are those who seem to want to believe but can only confess that they've never had a psychic experience themselves. While insisting that they accept psychism as a real phenomenon, they never consider pursuing it further! Some have heard friends speak of their own experiences, and while they don't dismiss these encounters, they tend to end their accounts of them with, 'I don't really know what to think about that.' They are an interesting lot. I believe these people have the ability to be psychic – perhaps more than most – but have chosen to be too 'busy', running their lives on rails, holding on to the inbuilt fears of their belief systems. Any psychic experience they did have would probably send them into crisis, as the mind has a way of protecting itself from what it is not ready to hear.

It is my belief that psychic ability runs in the genes and so can be a characteristic of particular families. My own mother had the ability to 'sense' and 'see', and she often had dream visions giving her important messages. My father, an intensely practical man who throughout my childhood tried to stop me 'dabbling', as he put it, confessed a few years after my mother's passing that he had had some staggeringly powerful psychic experiences. Of course, given his earlier attitude, I was amazed at his change of heart, but felt deeply touched that he had finally shared all that had happened and greatly respected his courage in doing so.

A BIT OF BACKGROUND

Being psychic and using psychic powers has a venerable and ancient history. Since time began, people have wanted to know what the future holds, seeking auspicious times to plant their crops and move their cattle, to make war, and to marry and merge dynasties. Whether seeking the answers to such questions by means of the sun, moon and stars, as with astrology; or via the flight path of geese, the entrails of a bull, or an oracle, as did the Greeks and Romans, those who developed and practised such arts were held in very high esteem, revered and set apart from all others through secret teachings and esoteric education.

Divination itself can be traced back to more than 2,000 years before Christianity. It was closely allied to the early Greek philosophers, whose wisdom and knowledge has been the foundation of so many erudite schools of learning. Aristotle, Paracelsus and Hispanus all had faith in psychism, and were themselves taught by Egyptian adepts whose mystery schools lodged a deep knowledge of truth and the nature of the afterlife, along with a staggering awareness of mathematics, astronomy and astrology. Then there was Pythagoras, who taught that numbers (numerology) can define the entire universe, with each base number of one through nine having a unique frequency and a value comprised of sound, colour and shape.

So the desire to know through divination goes back millennia. But who first taught the earliest teachers? Mustn't there have been someone or something before them to offer these teachings? I do not know, but many suspect there may have been an intelligence that visited earth and shared crucial information with a relatively small number of people who could take in and absorb such knowledge at the time. I am still questioning and researching some of the works in Egypt and India on the subject of ancient knowledge. It is interesting to note that the ancient divination sites were established at sacred places only one degree of latitude apart: Dodona lies at 39 degrees 30 minutes, Delphi at 38 degrees 30 minutes and Delos at 37 degrees 30 minutes, and there are matching sites in Asia and even on the slopes of Mount Ararat in Armenia. Why so? I'd love to know the answer. According to modern experts, such staggering and deliberate accuracy in the placement of these sites would have been quite beyond the knowledge or ability of the peoples living at the time

– but no doubt the same modern experts can't work out how the extraordinary mathematics of Pythagoras or the construction of the Pyramids was achieved back then either.

Perhaps the most famous of the divination sites is the Oracle in Delphi, Greece, where it is said the sun god Apollo resided. Apollo had among the widest ranges of divine attributes, being the god of music, truth and prophecy, and the patron of medicine. Cassandra, the daughter of King Priam of Troy, became one of his lovers, and in return Apollo offered her the gift of prophecy. But she later became unfaithful and from then on Apollo ensured her prophecies would never be believed.

Demand for the Delphic Oracle grew over the centuries, to the extent that sittings were increased from once to nine times a year, between February and October on the seventh day of each month. Sometimes as many as three Pythia (the name possibly derived from the Greek *pynthanomai*, meaning 'to ask') were working in shifts, and a special mass oracle was held annually on the Temple steps to ensure that the common people had access to the god as well. Everyone wanted their chance. But even then an audience with the Pythia was not guaranteed – supplicants had to undergo a series of tests to qualify for a consultation.

Whatever the Oracle did or did not reveal to those who were successful, there is certainly a place at Delphi which, in my experience, holds undeniable power. In this single spot I had an experience of 'the third kind' when I visited Delphi a few years ago, finding myself suddenly in a trance-like state. When I became conscious again, over an hour had passed. Everyone else had gone and there was just a peaceful silence. What I had lost in time I gained in knowledge.

Several years ago, two scientists spent time investigating the Delphic Sun Temple. They came up with evidence of vapours rising from a crevice underground. This they proposed was the cause of the nauseous trance-like state that the Oracle was reported to induce in the Pythia.

Personally, I did not require any such fumes to go into my trance at Delphi, but I believe that many of the ancient sites across the world were deliberately chosen and built upon for the immense energy they hold. That these energies align with potential geomagnetic stress points has now been scientifically ascertained, but what hasn't yet been generally accepted or understood is that these fields are significant gateways between our world and other dimensions, as I believe them to be.

King Croesus, Julius Caesar, Tiberius – all were entranced by omens and oracles. So was Alexander the Great. He retained a strong mystical streak, supposedly derived from his mother, the witch Olympias, whom he loved, hated, reviled and worshipped by turns during his short life (he passed over at the age of 33). It was she that convinced him of his divine power from the first, leading him to believe he was the undoubted descendant, or even reincarnation, of Achilles. Alexander's later successes on the battlefields of Asia only added to this conviction. Wherever he went, he sought out oracular sites, at times risking life and limb to find them and learn more.

But with the onset of organised religion all such arcane knowledge was deliberately suppressed. As early as AD 315 the Ecclesiastical Court passed an edict punishing anyone found practising 'outside the church' with excommunication and even death. Later, Henry VIII's Church of England ruled that all occult subjects were henceforth deemed witchcraft and sorcery. Such laws have led to fears that still resonate today in the psyche of the Christian Church.

So the once noble art of divination was forced underground

and became an occult practice, to be proclaimed only by witches or pilloried as a joke in carnivals or fairgrounds. But it never disappeared entirely. For example the sixteenth-century doctor and astrologer Nostradamus is still well known today in connection with prophecy. For me, Nostradamus can readily be defined as a seer – that is, someone who can tune into a certain brainwave frequency at will in order to see visions of the future. In his time he was at once revered, feared and held in high esteem. But his visions were not always acceptable in their purest form and had to be disguised or couched in more cryptic ways that left them open to wider interpretation. It seems that few of the living could readily accept what was 'seen' or, as I prefer to put it, 'written' in advance of its due time.

In modern times, some national leaders, such as former US president Ronald Reagan, have again turned to divination for guidance, even if they have kept their potentially controversial psychic interests somewhat in the closet. As a subaltern, in his younger days, Winston Churchill made a connection with a famous medium in Cairo. Later, during times of important decision-making during World War Two, including the setting of the timetable for D-day, he continued to keep this line of communication open and use it. By then, he had been made well aware by the British intelligence services that Hitler himself had relied heavily on an astrologer and a medium both before and at the outset of war – although I have no doubt that he never heeded the warnings he received about the nefarious course he was taking.

Be it the Druids, twelfth-century Catholic prophet St Malachi, sixteenth-century English prophet Mother Shipton, Elizabethan magician John Dee, the charismatic and controversial Russian healer Rasputin, or twentieth-century American psychics Edgar Cayce and Jeanne Dixon, it seems that those with the gift of 'sight' remain the object of our fascination. For most of us the idea of seeing the future through divination, omen and prophecy is intriguing. We still read the horoscopes in the dailies and in women's magazines. We still want to know about our love lives, our careers, our relationships, our money and our family members, whether living or dead. And many of us will have experienced 'coincidences' that leave us feeling inexplicably that we knew they would happen or that the gods must have been smiling on us for them to take place, as if they were proof positive that we are on the right path.

THE POWER IN THE MIND

Personally, I much prefer the word 'sensitive' to 'psychic'. For me it encompasses a far broader spectrum of understanding. After all, if you are 'sensitive', it stands to reason that you literally 'sense' more and are affected by what you sense more than most. I firmly believe that there is a further function in the brain that in most of us lies dormant unless consciously activated – in the right brain for those who are right-handed, the left brain for those who are left-handed. A sensitive is born with this brain function already switched on. Let me give you an example.

Boris Kipriyanovich was born in Volzhsky, Russia, in 1996. By the age of eight months he was speaking whole phrases and making geometrically correct structures using his toy Meccano set. Remarkable enough perhaps, but by the age of three he was telling his parents about the universe and naming all the planets correctly, even their satellites. He followed up with the names and numbers of the many galaxies. He also talked about extraterrestrial civilisations and the existence of an ancient human race three metres tall.

As time went on, Boris's mother grew increasingly worried by his apparent special abilities. She decided to check whether the astronomical information he was giving was accurate. Imagine her shock when the astronomy text books proved that he was absolutely correct!

Unsurprisingly, Boris quickly became a local celebrity. Everyone wanted to understand how he could know so many things – even if they didn't believe some of his less verifiable, science-fiction-like stories.

Eventually, Boris was baptised. From then on, he began to point out people's sins and warn them of troubles and diseases ahead. Of course, much of this information was just a bit too close too home, and his parents' standing in the community quickly plummeted. All the same, the world's leading space agencies say that young Boris knows information about Mars that he cannot actually know. His mother says:

> When we showed our boy to a variety of scientists, astronomers and historians, including ufologists, all of them agreed that it would be impossible for him to make all those stories up. The foreign languages and scientific terms that he uses are usually used by specialists studying this or that particular science.

So is Boris a savant, a psychic or a sensitive? To me he can only be a sensitive, one born with the ability to use the further brain function that most of us can only cultivate.

USING TOOLS

There are many ways in which a psychic or sensitive can work. To me, the true medium needs nothing more than themselves to work properly, but this requires a certain 'completeness' from within, together with a love and total trust of self. That said, many very competent psychics regularly use tools, and a sensitive can display exceptional talent when working with one. Such tools help them to discipline their minds and focus accurately enough to hear messages from the other side clearly or to see visions of the past, present or future. Whichever tools you try, the trick is to find one that you feel comfortable with then learn how best to work with it and interpret the information it gives you.

While I personally consider all tools to be props, I do not intend this in any pejorative way – people should suit themselves. And the list of possible props is enormous. There are Tarot cards, tea-leaves, runes, bones, angel cards, pendulums, crystal balls, coffee-grouts, pieces of paper, pebbles, even sand – far too many options to go into in detail in this book. Of the more usual working methods, astrology, graphology and numerology can be extremely effective. While one can use these tools without being a sensitive, I believe that a diviner is better equipped when they use their sixth sense. In my experience, intuition greatly enhances one's ability and accuracy.

Although I don't use it much now, I began with palmistry as my tool. It was my first study in childhood, thanks to a wonderful old book I came across and 'borrowed'. So while my school friends were learning all the dull, ordinary subjects, I was deeply immersed in the ancient work of *Scientific Palmistry* – and then busily trying it out on all my friends and family.

There is evidence of the use of palmistry, or chiromancy ('hand-reading' in Greek), dating back thousands of years. The Ecclesiastical Court of AD 315, mentioned on page 7, threatened any person caught practising it with excommunication or death, while in the 1600s James I ordered that the words 'God gave the seal in man's hand in order that he may know his work' be removed from the new King James edition of the Bible.

In the early 1900s, Cheiro, a well-known adept in palmistry from the UK, came across an ancient book on the subject in a cave in Hindustan, in northern India. It was written on animal, or possibly even human, skin in a rare red ink and was being guarded by Brahmins. He wrote about his experiences in detail in the book *Palmistry for All*. At around the same time, Sir Charles Bell – well known in his time for his work on nerve connections – noted that there were more nerves running from the brain to the hand than to any other portion of the body. He deduced that as the action of the mind affects the whole system it therefore followed that every thought must more immediately affect the hand.

I became so good at practising my new passion that people were spooked. My reputation must have spread because when I was 17 years old my mother got a call from our local vicar asking if I would stand in for 'Madame Mono' in the fortune-teller's booth at the village fete. I was ecstatic. I took it very seriously. Dressed up as a gypsy, I promptly reported to the tent at the bottom of the vicarage garden. I told fortunes there for three hours, and goodness knows how many people I saw (the queue seemed endless), but again and again they asked me, 'How do you know all this when you're not even looking at my palm?'

Of course, I didn't know the answer at the time, but after that I was booked for the village and church fetes annually, and I went on to do various prominent charity events in London and the south of England. It was all such fun, but somehow I always became ill afterwards, suffering either nausea or a bad migraine. Back then I knew nothing about psychic protection. I didn't realise you had to 'tune in' and then 'tune out' once you'd finished reading, so without being aware of it I was literally draining my own energy field! But each step is a learning. In this book, I will be showing you how to take some simple steps to ensure that this doesn't happen to you. You can probably remember occasions yourself when someone you know poured out all their worries to you and then said they felt so much better – while you ended up feeling tired and listless after they had gone ... I call that 'dumping'.

As I have said, this book is intended to give you the skills to access the psychic power of your conscious mind without the use of tools, but before we start to do just that, there is one intriguing psychic tool that I feel should be covered in some detail.

The naadi palm leaves

The most exciting and amazing evidence of ancient predictions that I have come across to date is the naadi palm leaves – 'palm' here referring to the tree rather than the palm of the hand. The general term 'naadi reader' is actually quite common in India and is widely used in the same way we speak of a psychic reader. The particular sect of naadi palm leaf readers I am referring to, however, are located in the state of Tamil Nadu, in south-east India, where they continue an ancient prediction practice (one of the meanings of *naadi* in Tamil is 'in pursuit' or 'in search of'). I was told about them by a friend, just before I first visited India with my husband, Andrew.

The naadi palm leaves are scripted leaves dating back more than 2,000 years and including predictions for humanity during the time we now live in. But if that is not mind-boggling enough, the existing leaves are copies of originals written in peacock's blood on animal skin at a much earlier date. These earlier leaves were written in Sanskrit and were translated into Tamil from the original Sanskrit on the order of a Chola king of southern India and then stored in the palaces of the kings called Sarawati Maha. It is held that Lord Shiva first spoke the words inscribed there 5,000 years ago and that they come from the Akashic records (held on all human, animal and other life forms).

Since then, generations of holy men have been taught how to read and interpret the leaves, which are grouped into 108 basic categories, with each category corresponding to specific markings found on the seeker's thumb. The leaves hold prophecies only for those who are destined (as foreseen by the rishis, the ancient Hindu holy men) to seek out their predictions. Should your thumb-print be found to match one of the categories of leaves, the current holy men will advise you in great detail on the progress of your soul through life.

The ancient rishis believed that there is rebirth for all souls except those that have progressed far enough to attain complete liberation. It is said that those who have reached this stage of progression will have been aware of it throughout their life – since well before their actual reading. It is also said that they will not be found unless it is their due time to be read.

Personally, I found receiving a reading from the naadi leaves an awesome and uplifting experience. It gave me confirmation of all I believed about my current life's journey and strengthened my resolve. For my husband, however, the experience was more shocking. He was incredulous when, from nothing more than his thumb-print, a complete stranger who didn't speak any English told him (via a translator) all the significant details of his life up to that moment, including information about his background and education, and the names of his family members. The reader went on to tell him about his career and personal life ahead, year by year. He also told him that his mother was seriously ill at that moment but would pull through, so when we arrived back at our hotel that night to receive the message at the desk, 'Urgent, your mother is dangerously ill. Please fly home', it just about finished him off!

If you are interested in the naadi leaves, let me issue a word of warning. In my experience, only a small group of holy men is following these ancient predictive traditions and using them with the highest spiritual integrity. As with so many other psychic and spiritual practices in the world today there are always unscrupulous opportunists around, just waiting to take your money. Please be cautious and search out those who are genuine.

STAYING SAFE

There are some simple guidelines for staying safe while doing psychic work. Never put yourself in a situation that feels dangerous – even a little. Never work with a person (or people) who makes you feel uneasy – especially if you are doing advanced training in mediumship, such as trance work. Trust your own sense, not what others tell you. When you have completed the training covered in this book, you will have a good understanding of psychism and the ability to be in control. You will also have built up your self-worth enough to trust your own intuition.

Through experience comes knowledge, but be aware from the start that on the other side there are many levels. Creatures, beings and people all reside in spirit form but all are where they are best suited to be, mixing only with their own kind. Those dwelling on the higher levels possess great beauty, love and harmony. They are concerned with helping all to progress for the highest good. Those on the lowers levels, however, are more physical, brutish and material by nature. The lower the level, the more dense, dark and heavy the energy becomes. But don't worry – there are specific ways of protecting yourself, which I will be covering in detail later in the book.

The ouija board

There is one, to my mind, very dangerous psychic tool that I feel deserves some more detailed words of caution. It is one that will be familiar to people of every age and creed, and for some, no doubt, that familiarity will be tinged with fear and real regret. Unfortunately, through naivety, it is via the ouija board that many people – especially children and teenagers – first experience communication with the other side. Almost all of these people will have been completely unaware of how vast and perilous the expanse that exists out there in the beyond.

In my opinion 'player beware' should be printed in very large letters on every ouija board box, for this is a tool by which the player is seduced as glibly as they are informed, and trapped as easily as they are teased with more and more accurate personal information, tugged slowly and deliberately down a slippery slope that knows no pleasant or easy end. An old-fashioned instrument, it has survived by its very success at gulling the innocent into entering its own dimension, where it alone has total control. Sadly, many continue to use it, refusing to believe that there is any danger to themselves or their state of mind.

Think of modern technology – radio, mobile phones, PCs, Broadband, Bluetooth, DVD, TV and so on. These are all wonderful tools of communication, and they all have one saving grace. You can turn them off. Not so with the ouija board, at least not without serious experienced help. From the day you make that first 'call' the line of communication is open, and will be deliberately held open at the other end.

To begin with, the ouija board works on sheer human desire together with the physical touch of two or more people. It then acts like a telephone circuit. Once dialled up, so to speak, a hole like a vortex is created, through which the players' questions will resonate like a tannoy. While time and distance may mean something in this world, they certainly do not on the other side of the vortex. There, all existence can hear, and there are plenty of ghosts and entities just waiting to pop through and keep you company. Believe me, they can pick up everything about you from your energy field – your work, your likes and dislikes, your ambitions, your family, your friends, your whole life. This is exactly what they thrive on. Regrettably, unless you are highly trained in 'opening up' and 'closing down' and are always working in a positive manner and in full control, these beings will arrive thick and fast, vying for a chance to feed off your curiosity, vulnerability and fear.

Their siren calls start gently, by way of a simple and apparently innocuous response to your enquiry – we humans are so easy to trick. Then they gain your confidence bit by bit by telling you a few truths; giving you the names of people connected to you; telling you about your past, your present and then your future. They start with minor things that will happen in a few days' time . . . and it all sounds so harmless, so good, so positive and exciting. But it won't be long before you are hooked and can't resist hearing more, and that is when the fun really starts. Suddenly things begins to turn nasty. You are given more and more unpleasant predictions, which quickly escalates into information about accidents one of you is going to have – that is, if you're lucky. Death is always predicted, and if you can't stop yourself asking when and how (and who could in the circum-stances?), they will very authoritatively give you all the details and the date on which it will happen. All such great fun – for them.

Tell-tale signs of disturbance will start to appear in your property too – cold spots, sounds of heavy breathing, the feeling that someone is watching you, objects being thrown about, dark shadows that can be seen out of the corner of your eye, random electrical surges, smells, noises and mechanical malfunctions. Some entities will enjoy picking on one of you in particular – the one who is more fearful, quiet or reticent, to whom it can most easily attach itself, as will then be evidenced by the headaches, weakness, depression and sickness that that person will suffer from.

I started playing with the ouija board in my teens with a French girlfriend called Gigi. After three goes in one week, strange happenings started to take place in my home. My mother came downstairs one morning to find devastation – smashed objects lying on the landing, bits of a vase on the stairs and broken objects all over the sitting-room, where we'd been using the board. Then my sister (who knew nothing of the games we were playing) confessed she had felt a presence in her room at night: she had heard heavy breathing, then the bedspread had been pulled off the bed while she was in it and the curtains blown around as though the windows were open to a great gale. She was absolutely petrified by it all.

The ghost person who was communicating then boasted to Gigi and me that it was he that had caused the breakages, crow-ing that we couldn't stop him. Then he told us who we were going to meet the following weekend, with their names, ages and personal details – and indeed we did meet these people! But then came the part when we were told, 'You are going to die', and if that wasn't bad enough at our tender age, which of our friends would have a serious accident – which took place within days.

So please don't do it. Do not buy a ouija board – you'll regret it. And never, ever let children, of any age, play with one. Believe me, I've had to pick up the pieces too many times.

THE POWER IN ALL OF US

On a happier note, I believe we all have the ability to activate the dormant psychic power that lies inside each of us, and to work with it properly and beneficially. Unfortunately, fear of this power has been handed down from our elders and is ingrained in many of us. Clients frequently say they are fascinated and would love to learn more about my work but that they feel too frightened to do so due to their education or past conditioning. It is my opinion that if you are drawn to a subject, you should check it out, learn all about it and go on from there. Sensitives are simply those who have realised and manifested the ability to pick up vibrations, sounds and visions undetected by most human beings. Rather like a radio or TV receiver, they have developed an active aerial that can be directed to work beneficially in their own lives as well as those of others.

I believe that if the childhood of a sensitive has been warm, loving and happy, their gift will naturally manifest in the most positive of ways. In my own childhood, my relationship with my twin sister always supported my psychic ability. We had a strong telepathic link throughout our childhood and on into adulthood – there was never any doubt when either or us communicated mind to mind with our thoughts and visions. Equally, I believe that a sensitive who has had a suppressed or unhappy childhood is likely to block any facility that could become active. That said, a greater part of life's journey is learning to act, or react, positively in any and every adversity, and I know of many who have worked through and healed their past and gone on to enjoy successful careers and happy lives using the psychic protocols I have taught them.

But however fortunate their background, to be completely effective sensitives still need to learn how to work their innate power by way of true will. By 'true will' I refer to the ability to act or refrain from acting at any one time. This involves arresting the idle, automatic and endless chatter emanating from the subconscious area of the brain, with the result that the sensitive is in overall control and nervousness and fear do not prevail. Without true will, all that will be received are fogged images and unclear sounds on a hit-and-miss basis at best. But I will deal with this in more detail later.

PSYCHICS AND TV

I'm often asked why it is that the psychics always seem to do so badly in the parapsychology tests that are occasionally shown on TV (usually during prime time on Sundays, of course) so let me tell you what I think.

The Independent Television Commission (ITC), the UK's regulatory board for television, insists that scientists and other experts are booked for programmes on the paranormal in order to give a balanced view. However, it appears to me that, knowingly or not, time and again these experts create blocks that invalidate the tests. In my personal experience, the nature of the tests is always determined by scientists' particular way of thinking, which results in trials that are too rigidly and tightly defined. It's a bit like trying to explain radio or electricity to scientists in the seventeenth century – they may sense that such things are a possibility, but as yet they have neither the understanding nor the methods by which to translate them into their own experience.

If the sensitive is unduly nervous or has difficulty in controlling subconscious chatter, so bringing in their 'what if' fears as well, it only adds to the problems. The human mind is readily capable of creating negative blocks. If these are allowed to take hold, they will without a shadow of doubt obstruct any sensitive trying to do their work. I believe that this is a major reason why so many 'scientific' tests fail to demonstrate a true sensitive's powers.

Remember, too, if it's TV there's always a sceptic lurking about and while, in the current climate of thought, even scientists have to accept that psychic powers can be neither proved nor disproved, it doesn't stop them trying, even if 'proof' consists only of rehashing or re-running tests they have already been using for far too long. But as far as the TV companies are concerned, it's all 'entertainment'.

Unfortunately, this approach places the poor spot-lit psychic on the stage as little more than a trained freak or performing animal, rather than a well-intentioned person intent on demonstrating their gift before the public at large, an approach that inevitably leads to the repetition of more and more inconclusive experiments. Can the spirit ever be put in the bottle for all to see?

Not that I'm saying some so-called psychics don't deserve to be exposed in this way, but given the current mindset of most scientists (and nearly all TV companies, which, in my opinion, seek confrontation rather than true evidence) the tarnished reputation of one then happily determines the general reputation of all.

At the very least, the controlling scientist or psychologist should be kept well away from the psychic(s) while the tests are being carried out. Evidence at Stanford University, in the USA, has demonstrated that a non-believer naturally creates a negative field around unsuspecting students with potential psychic ability that can and will inhibit positive results. This to me is enough evidence in itself. The power of the mind is such that humans can cause destructive havoc through their own personal beliefs – sometimes without realising it perhaps, but sometimes, I am sure, entirely deliberately. Scientists have fears too.

HOW TO RECOGNISE THE REAL THING

Unfortunately, there are some who see psychic ability as a quick way to fame and material wealth and seem happy to waste their lives trying to achieve it by faking and deceiving themselves. They capitalise upon the innocence (and sometimes the desperation) of others and believe they can make a name for themselves by spouting what people want or expect to hear in sound-bites at regular intervals. These people do not give true messages from beyond at all.

I believe that the best way to recognise a genuine psychic is through personal recommendations from those you trust and/ or your own observations – i.e. what you see, hear and sense when a psychic is working, be it with you personally or on stage or TV. I am frequently impressed by the awareness of the seekers I meet, who generally pick up straightaway whether a medium is really good. While there are showmen in every field, it is usually not difficult to suss out the genuine sensitive who speaks and works with integrity, doesn't try to impress or curry false favour with the audience, and simply and honestly gives the questioner the information they are receiving as best they can. Remember, a psychic is there to give messages to assist you, not to act as if they're a god. A little genuine humility speaks volumes over a fancy outfit and eye-catching accessories, which dazzle for a reason.

A couple of years ago, I stopped my car on the spur of the moment because I had seen a 'psychic gypsy' offering readings at the roadside. Her ability was definitely lacking, however, and when I asked her where she thought she was getting her information from, she had no answer that made any sense to me. Then she asked me if I could help her, and I ended up giving her a full-length reading. She then had the cheek to charge me for her time. Don't ask who eventually coughed up the money!

That said, I've come across many the genuine article in many situations, often where I've least expected to find it – for instance at a number of summer shows, and even once at the local fairground. With a little practice you'll soon learn to recognise who's doing what and why. A good lawyer can be harder to find!

RECEIVING DIFFERENT READINGS FROM DIFFERENT PSYCHICS

This is another favourite disproof of psychism with scientists, who expect to repeat each and every experiment with exactly the same results every time. Without this consistency, they cannot accept that psychism has been proven as credible and therefore scientifically acceptable.

For me, inconsistency in readings is all about human fallibility. I do not judge others, but it should be remembered that we humans vary greatly and all of us are at different stages of development and soul progression. This includes psychics. Some will see only past events; some will see what is going on in the here-and-now, take it to mean the future and then make assumptions, while still others will hear and use reason and logic to create the big picture by surrendering to their imagination.

Being only human like everyone else, psychics can feel under great pressure to perform and may well have problems in their own lives or even feel ill. All of these things can create negative influences or, much worse, cause the sensitive to become negative in their outlook on life, which will naturally affect their approach to any reading they give.

It is also human nature to judge appearances and attitudes, and unless the psychic has progressed far enough to disregard these things, they may rely too heavily on their impression of what and who they see walking in – the way they look, how they speak and what they say on arrival. A great rule – one I have always kept to – is that when someone comes in they must simply sit down and keep quiet. The only thing I allow them to talk about is the weather. Once I start the reading, they are allowed to interject with a brief 'yes' or 'no', but no more. All conversation is forbidden until I have finished reading and tuned out.

Even for the skilled reader, there may still be times when psychic information is simply not forthcoming. I remember one particular lady who came to see me. She walked in and sat down, and I tuned in. Nothing! I received no message whatsoever. I kept re-tuning but each time only got a denser and denser field around not only her, but which spilled out and emanated around the room as well. After a little while, I gave in, apologised to her and told her the truth: 'There is a terribly dense negative fog around you, and there is nobody in spirit coming through. It's just as if the phone lines have gone down.' To which she responded, 'Well, I'm not at all surprised. I've been in such a black depression I could actually feel a smog around me, and I just can't seem to get rid of it.'

The effects of depression and other negative states of mind should not be underestimated. The human body exudes a life force, generally referred to as your 'energy field', to a lesser or greater extent. According to a report in *Discovery News*, a recent study at the Central Research Laboratory, in Japan, found that hands, foreheads and parts of the foot emit light by releasing photons. These photons were measured and were found to be lacking in strength whenever a person was suffering from negative states such as stress, fear, unhappiness, anger and so on. So thoughts and emotions will have an effect. I'll explain more about this in Chapter Four.

PSYCHIC POWER AND SPIRITUALITY

Does religion matter if you are involved in psychic work? No. I believe all spokes of the wheel lead to the same centre, the same spiritual hub, and this hub is there for all living things (including animals and plants) irrespective of their chosen spiritual path. After death, realisation comes to us by right of passage. We naturally tap straight into the fount of knowledge held by the source in the universe, and then each of us, and each of us alone, becomes the judge of our own life and our own actions.

Maintaining balance in life and endeavouring to keep a balanced view is undoubtedly a hard road to follow. The true will required to do so demands great effort – and in turn great energy. However, when any human being chooses to cross the line and take an extreme path in any area of their lives – be it in the area of alcohol, work, sex, religion, sport, financial gain or whatever – an equivalent weakness is created in another area, which will perforce affect harmony and balance overall. You will not make a good psychic if you are not already in harmony with yourself, integrated and with a deep love for the planet.

If we could only all enjoy life and resonate with our beautiful Earth then we could comprehend the absolute importance of living without causing suffering. Yet it seems it is only through sadness that we begin to learn to recognise happiness. Our forefathers led us into fear and guilt with the religions and rules they created, all of which still press down on us greatly. I believe the true source to be much more forgiving.

Any sensitive that is true to themselves can feel the suffering in the world. The only true sin we are guilty of is the suffering and pain that we as individuals cause to other human beings and life forms. This, I know, ricochets backwards and forwards, and results in the soul suffering self-imposed pain for what will seem like an eternity in the afterlife awaiting all of us. The pain I pick up from cruelly treated animals – let alone human beings – is absolutely immense, and sometimes almost unbearable if I don't manage to control my reaction to it. So we must all look within for the suffering we create, whether out of ignorance or out of madness, for we are each accountable for our actions when we ultimately re-attach to what I term the 'spirit net'.

There are over 220 religions in existence in the world today, each of them born out of a different race and community. But it is spirituality rather than religion that is vital if you wish to be a good psychic. This means having the ability to empathise with the ideas and attitudes of other people, and trusting in your own sense, rather than what you were conditioned or educated to believe as a child. There is far more out there than the orthodox religions in terms of trust and faith, and there are definitely those of us who would prefer us not to find or know it. Aeons may be needed for the consciousness of humankind to comprehend the full potential of all I am telling you right now. And if we did comprehend it, political and religious leaders (some of whom are well aware of how much more is kept buried in history) would simply lose their control over the rest of us. So it seems to me that, if anything, they would wish to slow down the learning and dissemination of this knowledge. If we are all kept busy in the usual ways, it is much easier for them to stay in power.

So whatever belief system you are happy following, remember that the spirit net is non-denominational and filled with boundless love and good wishes. Happiness and joy can only come with a positive outlook on life in general, and if you can truly connect to your very being – your essence, your soul – and love and forgive yourself, then your positive energy will resonate out in the world, sending amazing, glowing signals of love and joy to all around. It sounds sweet and sentimental I know, but just try it and see what you get back. It works.

I have used the word 'spirituality', but you should be aware that in both orthodox and psychic terms a 'spiritualist' is one who belongs to or follows the Spiritualist Church, which was founded in the UK but now has a world-wide following and is a recognised religion. Spiritualists hold that giving evidence of life after death is of primary importance. Their rules and regulations state, however, that they may not give out any information on the future (despite the fact that this is precisely what many people want to hear).

It was on this count that, on one occasion, I caused a medium at the Spiritualist headquarters, in London, a great deal of embarrassment some years ago while having a sitting. The medium sat me down in a tiny room where there were two chairs and a small table a few feet away. He was in the middle of the sitting when the table started to lift up and down, continually banging the floor. I really wanted to start laughing but managed to contain myself by biting my lip. Then, suddenly, he said, 'I can't carry on like this; there's a lady here who says she's your aunt and she won't stop banging the table until I tell you what's going to happen to the family in the future . . . Oh dear, but that's the one thing I'm not allowed to do!'

At that point I did laugh. The aunt was actually my Great-aunt Julia, who had always seemed ancient to me and who had passed over in the early 1980s at the ripe old age of 99. She had been one of the real old school psychics and an ardent spiritualist. Since then she'd always moved objects – tables, ornaments, glass ashtrays and so on. It was her way of attracting our attention at home. In life, she had always known what was going to happen in the family, and took great delight in informing everyone of her precognitive visions. As a child, I had always enjoyed it when she came to stay – she could read the tea-leaves like no other I have come across since, always giving accurate predictions, and I have never forgotten the wonderful spooky secrets she very determinedly wanted to share.

This and many other experiences have taught me that man-made restrictions on the work of a true sensitive should and need not apply. Be faithful to yourself and have integrity, but allow those with more wisdom than us mortals to show you the way towards spiritual progress and the future.

REMAINING POSITIVE AROUND NON-BELIEVERS

On a number of occasions, I have been approached without warning and ridiculed by those who hold a sceptical view of psychism or work for a body that does. They have apparently been unable to stop themselves attacking me verbally, sometimes very aggressively, without any provocation whatsoever, usually while I am pinned down at a charity function, or in a TV or radio studio. I find all this highly amusing, which no doubt only incenses them all the more. My policy is to remember the more we speak out, the more such sceptics will feel compelled to respond.

However, if you follow the training outlined in this book, and live with the power daily and call for like-minded people to be around in your life, you will soon find that such situations, should you encounter them, are really not intimidating.

THINGS THAT CAN BLOCK YOU

There are a few things, not mentioned so far, that I believe can block your opening up, preventing you from using your power fully.

First, sceptical people may choose to see your beliefs as a weakness, belittling you with their reactions or attitudes to what you are now doing. You have to realise that you cannot change another person's reactions, only your own. Many people consider 'sensitivity' (and similar forms of creativity) to be weak, not for any macho reasons but simply because they fear it.

Second, you may quite naturally have doubts about whether what you are hearing is actually spirits or just yourself. The better you learn to control your mind, the more you will perceive the difference between your own mental chatter and the real thing. Genuine psychic communication is achieved when your pure consciousness connects with your soul's personal 'tuning disc' – effectively your higher self – which is eternal. Don't worry – I'll be covering this in more depth later.

Third, ego has its place in the personality, but it needs to be kept firmly in check, otherwise it can balloon and warp, just like a plastic bag full of liquid. I call ego people 'the great I am's', for ego has a vast, greedy appetite. If you allow yourself to be too dominated by it, you will become opinionated and boastful of your worth. The ideal is to balance ego with empathy (i.e. to have your own self-worth). This allows you sensitivity towards other people's problems and situations so that you can relate to them, but without 'becoming' them or taking on their problems yourself. Remember, we all have our own journeys to take, and you can't take others' journeys for them, nor should you seek to do so.

The common factor in all three of these blocks is fear – the problem that all of humanity suffers from to a greater or lesser extent, and which quickly takes on an aggressive form when people feel threatened. Fear will greatly inhibit your spiritual progress and ultimate success if you let it. To help you identify some of the causes and consequences of fear, I have made the following list:

FEAR is the unknown.

FEAR is going into uncharted territory.

FEAR is based on what you have been told by others.

FEAR is held in your memory, therefore you believe it to be so.

FEAR stops you seeking further knowledge.

FEAR halts life's adventures.

FEAR can lead you down the pathway to guilt.

FEAR feeds self-doubt and chips away at your self-esteem.

FEAR threatens your belief system (i.e. your inner safety blanket).

FEAR is believing someone could steal your thunder.

OK, enough is enough! There is no need to be under the thumb of fear. Now let me help you maximise your positive potential instead.

If I told you that not only are you a part of the universe but that you are also fully connected to it and have complete access to it anytime, anywhere, then understandably you would want to know exactly what I meant. So let's say the universe holds the divine 'gene' that allows you anything you want – no if's or but's about it – whether you are intent on material desires or a seeker of wisdom and knowledge. Both will feed you in a certain sense: one with a merely physical food, limited to life's desires; the other with a spiritually progressive nourishment of unlimited proportions.

Now it may sound strange or harsh, but the universe truly doesn't care whether you are wealthy or poor, well dressed or in rags. It is your own thoughts and actions that create every cause and effect in your life, and if you can come to terms with your fears by understanding and overcoming them, then you can become your own creator, with the full benefit of all of the energy in the universe to help you. And that means feeling totally safe, self-confident and always in control. You can have anything and everything you wish to call into your life, but first of all you must consider your intentions. Why do you want it? How will it truly benefit your progress? Is it really what you need in order to become self-empowered, content and happy?

WAKE-UP CALL: **COUNTERACTING YOUR FEARS**

Once you know what your fears are based on, it is vital that you start implanting positive, optimistic new thoughts in your mind to counteract your age-old negative responses. This a simple exercise that will help you to do just that.

- When you have some quiet time to yourself, sit down with a pen and paper and think about how you truly wish to be from this moment on.

- When you are ready, write out your wishes as statements about yourself in the present tense. Keep it direct and simple. For example, you might write:
  - I am totally safe and protected in all I do.
  - My self-worth gives me daily power.
  - I am now doing the perfect work in my life.
  - I have an abundance of joy in my life.

  This writing is personal and private, so don't share it with anyone, as this will dissipate the energy and prevent your wishes from manifesting in your life.

- Read what you have written first thing every morning and last thing every night for two weeks. In addition during this time, simply remind yourself of your wishes once a day with a smile, then release them from your thoughts and carry on with whatever you were doing.

This exercise is the key to a positive shift – a shift that will in turn allow you to discover your full potential and experience an increasingly heightened sense of personal freedom. And in so doing, you will be connecting to the spirit net, to the dimension that exists unseen among us, beyond the physical but within the universe, and in which everything you could wish for is held. Once you have made this connection, you can afford to say no with good grace, refusing to be coerced, manipulated or dragged into duties and obligations that others seek to put upon you but which do not serve you. You are now your own person, in balance and harmony with all.

WAKE-UP CALL: **BASIC PROTECTION**

Like moths to the flame, when your frequency vibrates at a higher pitch and your energy increases, you will start attracting many who seem almost helplessly drawn towards you. Some you will be delighted to have in your life – like-minded people, positive new friends, and those ready to engage with you in stronger, more deeply bonded relationships. However, there will be others – in both the physical and the non-physical world – that you will be less willing to extend a welcome to, those who are upset, jealous or disturbed by your greater vibrating power. The ghost people and the lower forms will all be able to see or sense your growing, glowing field from afar. And, regrettably, their negative fields will feed and thrive off your positive field, sapping your energy and having a vacuum-like effect on you. So protecting yourself against these entities is a necessity and must become a natural part of your psychic activity.

In this exercise, we concentrate on protecting the most vulnerable region of your body, the solar plexus (the area around your middle, between the chest and the navel). You should do this exercise first thing every morning.

- Extend your hands, with the palms facing towards you, making the tips of the longest finger on each hand touch.

- Hold your hands 6 cm (3 in) away from your body, in line with the top of your thighs, and then slowly run them up the front of your body to your lips, just as if you were pulling up a zip.

- Touch your lips and wipe them 'clean', then take your hands away.

Now you're all zipped up, which means that your energy will be kept intact and no one will be able to suck it out during the day. Always do this exercise again after a taking a shower or bath or sleeping. It will really help to strengthen you and keep you whole.

PSYCHIC TAKEAWAY: INSPIRATIONAL MOMENTS

On a lighter note, try creating inspirational moments in each day of your life from this moment on. A positive thought released in the moment can be incredibly powerful in manifesting your wishes. Once a moment has passed you by, it has gone forever. Make the most of that moment.

Now, each day give yourself a treat. While waiting at the traffic lights, sitting at your desk or just walking, think of a delight, a surprise or an experience you would love to have ahead of you. Sense it in that moment, with a laugh or a smile.

This is a magical booster for the mind, body and soul. You are drawing something positive into your day. Try it and just see what happens.

The more people who do this daily, the greater the positive effect for all of us.

SIGNPOSTS IN MY LIFE 2

I believe we all come from spirit and go back to spirit, so to communicate with spirit while in the physical domain can only be greatly beneficial, however strange it may sound. Even if it does not appear to be in accordance with current scientific laws, I wish to help you access that spiritual potential, for there are mysterious forces that remain unknown to science.

I made a vow when I was 12 years old. I knew I had come into being for my last journey, and I was tired. As I precociously informed my mother at the time, 'I'm going to seek wisdom and knowledge throughout my life and share it with all those who are ready to know the truth.' I can still see my mother patting me gently and saying, 'Yes, darling,' in a condescending voice. The memory still makes me smile, but for many years such a life was just what I prayed for.

For the selling of this book, my agent, Susan, arranged meetings with four publishers in one day. Two of them were delightful, warm and very welcoming – you could say we connected on a number of levels virtually at once. The third was also encouraging but was slightly caught up in (or, you could say, boxed in by) 'the rules of the house', and I quickly sensed their restriction. The fourth one was from a well known major publishing house. When I walked into the building, the atmosphere was cold and sterile. The people and offices were smug and official-looking – so much so that I remarked to Susan it felt like the Inland Revenue! Of course, from that moment on the meeting could only go downhill, which it did.

Half an hour after the time of our appointment, I was still waiting to see the person we had come to meet, and so wished to leave, but Susan coaxed me into waiting a little longer. I stomped off to the bathroom, from where I heard Susan's voice speaking to someone. I walked out to meet the lady we had been waiting for. I shook hands but felt uneasy immediately – to me it was all over already. She took us for coffee and asked if I would like some chocolate, as she wanted some. I jumped at the idea (being a passionate chocolate-lover) and we sat down. Having waited until I had eaten most of the bar, she said curtly: 'I've read your synopsis. I know a lot about these subjects. What makes you think you know all about them? Who do you think you are?'

My mouth was still full of chocolate as she finished her timely assault. My mood and energy had already been dampened by her lateness. You can guess what I wanted to do. So I stood up and said politely: 'Forgive me, I think a mistake has been made. I am so sorry for wasting your time . . . and indeed mine,' and walked out, with Susan trying to catch me up.

In a way it was a good experience – all still more learning. But the reason I tell you this here is because I have not come into being to justify my life. I truly believe I came here to share the key I have found, and now is the time I must give that key to you so that you can try it out for yourself and seek your own evidence, no more and no less. It is always healthy to question, so question without fear.

MY EARLY SIGNS

When and how did my spiritual learning start? I believe the knowing (as I call it) was with me at birth. As I have said, I am a twin, and I was born first, as if I knew all about it, had been there, done that, etc., whereas my second-born twin suffered a trapped head and a few other minor mishaps. The hospital matron, wise old soul that she was, told our mother that I would always be the one 'out there' in life so she would never have to worry about me, but Engie, my twin, would always find it tough. Sadly, these words proved true.

I was three years old and it was a summer's day. My mother had told me to go and tell my father that lunch was ready – he was cutting back bamboo shoots down at the bottom of the driveway. As I wandered off to tell him, I stopped at a big tree outside the garden gate, from where I could see my father in the distance. As I stood there watching him, quite suddenly I heard a voice outside my head. It was a man's voice (not my father's), very calm, controlled and soft, and somehow very kind and good to hear. 'Angela,' it said. I looked around (including behind the tree) to see where the word had come from and who had spoken it, but there was no one.

'Angela,' it repeated. Then again, 'Angela.' Moments went by. I was flummoxed, but then I simply responded, 'Yes,' very quietly – and I knew then that it, or rather he, had gone.

Later, I told my mother what I'd heard. She said, 'Oh, did you, darling?' and quietly went on with what she was doing. But I never forgot that most beautiful voice calling me.

A few years after that I went to a convent school. When one of the nuns quoted, 'and God said to Moses' in one of our lessons, I stood up in class and excitedly told her, 'Please, Sister,

God has spoken to me as well!' Of course, I was ridiculed for saying such a stupid thing: 'What makes you think God would speak to you, you silly child?' she said haughtily. A good question indeed.

From the age of 11 onwards I was running ghost-hunts at our old home in Sussex during the school holidays, as well as trying to find the secret passage that the deeds of the house stated was 'one hundred paces from the lime walk', which had long since been buried.

At the age of 12, I started putting my wishes out there. They were all big wishes, of course, but all of them have come about, even though a couple of them took 20 years to come to fruition. For example, I wished for an amazing white horse that could leap and do amazing feats with me on its back; years later I got my Lipizzaner, one of the white dancing horses from Vienna, which I still have today. It was at this age, too, that I asked if I could leave school. I was sure it had taught me everything I needed to know and was finding the lessons so dreadfully dull! Silly as it may sound, I don't believe I really learnt much more of real value from then on anyway.

Telepathy

From very early on, telepathy was part of my life with my twin. We each knew about everything the other was going to do, long before the action. It was so much a part of our lives that we couldn't understand why our friends hadn't got it. We played with it, we tested it and we lived with it. Of course, playing with it caused a great deal of trouble at school, so eventually we were put in different classes, and I got known as the trouble-maker.

It is thanks to telepathy that I was able to stay consciously 'open'. Although I did not realise it fully at the time, I had been given one of the natural gifts of a sensitive, and it allowed me to receive incredible information almost continually. These were not messages from people in the physical world, but from those lofty beings we all left behind when we came into this life, those on the other side, the ones I call my spirit colleagues and teachers.

Whilst listening to my mother worrying about her sister one day, I was told by these beings to tell her, 'It's all right, Mummy. She's going to be all right. She won't be going until she's in middle age, and that's not now. It's not her time.' Years went by and this aunt passed over at the age of 54.

A natural bond with pets and other animals

I was born and bred with animals, and they are every bit as much a part of my being as people, if not more so. To me every dog, cat, horse – in fact all domesticated animals – can bond one on one, moulding seamlessly with an individual's energy field. Some animals are unable to connect to certain people, but there is always the right one for you somewhere. I have observed over the years how each cat is drawn to a specific person and nobody else gets a look-in, and a dog will seek only one master. Indeed, I would go further and say that there's only one person in the life-time of any animal. All other owners are surrogates. When the true owner becomes ill, that animal's energy field will resonate with the symptoms, causing the animal to react in an extremely disturbed manner. Some will pine very greatly when the owner passes over, their loss truly felt.

I once arrived home from work to have my mother tell me that my little dog, Bambi, had had a heart attack and the vet was just about to take him away. I ran to him. He was still warm but lying there apparently lifeless. I put my hands on him and 'called' with all the strength my heart and soul could muster for help to bring him back. I don't know how long I pleaded my case, but he woke up, picked up his head and looked straight up at me. I cried for joy. He lived another two years, to a time when I could accept and be more ready for his passing, so when that time finally came and he passed over, it was fine. As I was going to sleep that very night, I felt him jump up on my bed, walk up and lie down beside me as he usually did. I softly responded with the words, 'It's all right, Bambi. I'm with you.'

My first pony was also called Bambi (could it have been anything to do with Disney?). When I grew up and left home, we had to find him somewhere else to live. I refused to sell him; it had to be just a loan to a home I could fully approve. I went to him and made him a promise that he would come back to me in his old age and spend his retirement with me, whenever or however that would be. Years went by and eventually I was in the right place. I went and brought him back from his foster home. He lived to be 39 years old, a great age for a horse, and he kept his promise too: he passed over on the one and only day that I was at home that month, with my arms tightly around him.

EARLY EXPERIENCES

When I was 17, we lived in a huge old house with hardly any electricity. The winters were long, dark and cold, and often my twin sister Engie and I got so bored that we would sit opposite each other and send telepathic messages back and forth – most of them jokes, so all anyone else would have heard was our laughter ringing out at odd intervals! But on one occasion we stayed totally quiet and Engie fell asleep while I innocently went into a trance-like state. I didn't mean to, it just happened.

Suddenly, the room changed completely to one of sparse furnishings. Instead of Engie sitting opposite me, there was a man in a very gnarled and ancient, turned, dark wooden chair staring back at me. He got up and started pacing up and down the room, clearly in a terrible state. He told me his daughters were in danger. They had been due back the day before and he worried – no, knew – that something had happened to them. He was terribly distraught. Yet in another moment it was as if he already knew they were dead.

In that instant, I found myself back in full consciousness and gave a little scream – I suppose it was the shock – whereupon Engie woke up, not knowing a thing of what had taken place. But when I later described the gentleman to our mother she said, 'You've seen "him", haven't you?' She recognised the man, whom she had been seeing regularly at night walking through her bedroom in seventeenth-century costume with its fine ruffles. The chair I saw him sitting on I have yet to find in any antique shop to this day, but I know it exists somewhere, and I can't stop myself keeping an eye out for it. I suppose I secretly want to have it as my own piece of proof.

A few years later, I was invited by a girlfriend's mother to have tea with a well-known medium. Together with my friend and her fiancé David, an army captain (a great joker and certainly a non-believer), I arrived for tea. The medium was an incredible lady, larger than life in every sense of the phrase, who informed me at once that she could pick up everything through touching a person's hands. So when she held on tight to mine for a good few minutes after our arrival, I had to smile!

We were led into an enormous room for our tea, and I was placed with David and a vast plate of sandwiches at the opposite end from the medium. She was chatting away, but after a while I began to become quite oblivious to what was being said. Then I found myself becoming 'removed' from the proceedings. I put my cup down and realised my heart was slowing down. For a while I could feel every beat and my breathing had become so shallow that I wasn't sure I was even there at all any more. I was staring at the others all talking, but their voices were becoming more and more faint as I looked. I was still conscious and was telling myself I was all right, it wasn't a heart attack, when I suddenly noticed a group of people arrive through the wall. They were in Edwardian clothes, each of them looking very smart indeed. Then I heard our hostess say, 'Oh, don't worry about her, she's in trance. She's safe here. All that's supposed to happen.' Distantly I wondered whether she was talking about me. I don't know how long I went on watching these spirit people flouncing around the room, but eventually I made a conscious effort to pull myself back. Then it dawned on me that this was like the moment before death!

This medium was wonderful. She took me aside afterwards and explained many spiritual things that she had experienced. In her very matter-of-fact manner she told me her mother and grandmother regularly visited her in the evenings, when apparently they would both sit down and have a chat with her just as though they were still living, and would often tell her who was going to visit her over the course of the next week. Before I left, she insisted I tell her when it was going to be her time to pass over. I have never enjoyed answering that one.

What I would say now is that there are people I have encountered who have an incredible calm and 'knowing' about them. I perceive this in their voice and their transparent honesty. It is as though the heavens open and I hear what they wish to know. With love, I have learnt not to be the judge or juror when that happens and just tell them what I hear. I am pleased to add that often the messages I am given to relate are much more optimistic than the person's own expectations.

There was another medium who taught me a very great deal through her spirit guide, Chan. Her name was Doris Wood. I first met her when I was 19, and I visited her every year without fail until her passing, much later on. By the time I was 24, she had told me many details about my life and my spiritual journey. She gave me all the warnings I needed to know well in advance of time. Her accuracy was such that I have never expected any less from any other medium, and especially from my own spiritual endeavours. Sadly, (like you, I feel sure) I am too often disappointed with the standard of mediumship presently. Regrettably, so are our spirit friends.

A harsh lesson

I have experienced a number of seriously creepy happenings, and would even go so far as to call some of them evil. I am going to share only one with you now – telling tales about the darker side was not my reason for writing this book.

At the age of 20, I was invited away by my then boyfriend for my very first 'dirty weekend'. I'll call him John to spare his blushes. He was in the Royal Navy and I'd known him for some years. On this occasion, he'd booked us into a delightful old inn in a fairly remote part of Devon, in south-west England.

My mother had warned me to take precautions and insisted I take condoms with me because I wasn't on the pill. Highly embarrassed, I refused to go and buy them, so she went and bought them for me instead, and proceeded to put them in my suitcase hastily hidden in a paper bag.

After hours of driving, we arrived at this fantastic, secret place, had a great dinner and went straight to bed. Carefully preparing myself in the bathroom, I opened the paper bag and to my horror found only a packet of Rennies, the indigestion tablets! (I found out later my mother had gone to the village chemist and cryptically and quietly asked him, 'Please could I have a packet of "R...e...ns",' referring to the brand of condoms called Rendels in those days.) But in my ignorance and despair I decided it would probably work if I held my breath every time we had sex, and I promptly did exactly that.

All was well until I woke up. I wasn't myself at all. I had some kind of driving force pressuring me hard, not physically but mentally – I can't explain it any better than that. All I knew at the time was that I had to be completely alone. You can imagine what that did for our 'romantic' weekend. But, without knowing why, I was very serious about it, and told John I had to be on my own for a while. I don't think he could believe it, but I was so insistent that he reluctantly agreed to go off after breakfast and drive around, which he then did, saying he'd be back around lunchtime.

The hotel was in a small village, more a hamlet really. I walked out of the front door into the main road, which in reality was nothing more than a lane. It was a warm sunny autumnal morning, and as I turned to walk up the road, past a few other old houses, I began to notice that there were no people and no cars around, in fact no sounds at all – absolutely nothing. Not even a bird.

I stopped and looked back at the hotel to make sure it was still there(!) and then slowly walked on. I reasoned that the village must be a very quiet place at this time of year and maybe everyone was out or working and shopping in Plymouth, which wasn't very far away.

Halfway up the lane, I felt compelled to turn back, but as I started to do so I felt increasingly panicked, as though I was fighting an unseen force that was both pulling and pushing me forwards at the same time. I fought it hard. But part of me was also intrigued and wanted to go with it, so I kept telling myself not to be so stupid; it couldn't be anything; I was simply imagining it all.

By now I was back outside the hotel again, but having got there I became aware that I had to walk past it and head for the gate of the church, which was almost next door. As I put my hand on the gate a great shudder ripped through me.

I started to get frightened. There was still nobody around, but, taking comfort from the nearness of the hotel, I made myself believe there had to be somebody there, working in the kitchen, cleaning the bedrooms, laying the tables or doing at least something normal. And, after all, I was only visiting the church, so where was the harm in that?

Reason and logic took over – for a while – and slowly, stopping and starting, I made my way up the church path. But by now I could hardly breathe. My heart was beating harder and harder with every step as my anxiety increased. What was still drawing me on? Eventually, I made it to the outer porch door and very bravely put my hand on the heavy handle and turned it – only to jump back in shock. The most awful, agonised shrill screams and horrific groans were coming from deep inside the church. When I dared to look through the inner door, all I could see was a mass of ghastly, greenish-brown, slimy ghoul-like things writhing and clamouring to get at me. Terrified, I turned and ran for my life.

Once I got back outside the church gate, it was suddenly all over, as if a switch had been flicked off. I could hear the birds singing now, and a car even went past – the first I'd seen that morning. Recovering somewhat, I fought with myself about whether to go and tell the vicar so he could do something about his church, though I couldn't imagine quite what. But then I thought better of it. He'd think I was mad or – even worse – expect me to go back in there with him to show him what it was or somehow deal with it. No way!

To me, all that evil had been created by humankind at some time or other, whether through suffering, torture or hatred, and reinforced and built up over the centuries. What on earth had been done there to create such monstrous creatures?

Having later researched the church in question, I found out it was built on an energy line known as the St Michael line, which runs through England, starting at St Michael's Mount near Marazion, in Cornwall. Going back through the ages, many Christian churches have intentionally been built on this energy line (as on others), aligned specifically so that the altar is placed right on the line. This alignment enhances and increases the power that can be summoned up by the priest. Indeed, it is only the churches built in recent times that miss out on this great potential. In this instance, the church was at least 500 years old and shared its site with the ruins of a castle dating to the 1600s that boasted one of the most dreadful reputations for punishment, torture and hangings in the whole of England.

Luckily, such entities such as the ones I encountered can only work their dense negative influences by desperately trying to draw in their potential victims (i.e. unsuspecting or naive sensitives who happen to be in their proximity) through something much like a magnetic field. And I was certainly one of those naive sensitives!

I must add that I believe we are all drawn into specific circumstances or events in order to learn and increase our understanding, although it is not until after the experience is over that we can reflect and reach this realisation. When asked, my spirit teachers would only ever tell me that such experiences were all learning and necessary for my progress. Through that ghastly encounter – and others since – I have learnt to recognise the signs of malevolence and without fail then use my 'sense' to protect myself and trust in my true power. Trust me when I tell you that these things do all exist in the other dimension and at a level below that which we live in. As in this instance, at a specific time in the year a portal can open for a short period – it could be for only a day or two – and then 'they' can rush through, albeit that they are contained within a boundary, the area that was the last place they dwelled before dying and the place of their death.

So, once again, I would advise you always to go with your own intuitive sense and never deny yourself by allowing others to make decisions on your behalf. If you don't feel right about something, don't do it. Trust in your power.

(And by the way, condoms failing, holding my breath worked as well!)

Astral travelling

I started astral travelling when I was 22, and at the time had no idea what was happening to me.

As soon as I put my head on the pillow, a minuscule vibration would start, and then would only increase in intensity. No matter how much I turned or moved, it would always start again when I lay still. I would put the light on and check that no one was rocking my bed, but each time the vibration would start up again.

After a few nights of this, it happened that I picked up a magazine, flipped it open and came across a story about a house-wife who had had the same problem (while hoovering, would you believe?). After that, I felt quite happy about it all and decided to go with it.

Wow! In one moment I seemed to sink down through my physical body and then, in the next, shoot out of the top of my head. If that wasn't enough, I then started tearing through walls and flying around and about, arms by my sides, soaring here and there just like the child in *The Snowman*. After rushing around for a while like a kid with a fabulous new toy, I learnt that if I used a strong enough thought, I could target a place I wanted to visit and quickly go there, travelling a little bit lower than a helicopter.

My experiences expanded and deepened as I travelled more and more, free as a bird, throughout the universe. Then one night, my husband, Andrew, got up to go to the bathroom and in doing so accidentally woke me up. Unbeknown to him, at the time I was travelling way away beyond Earth, heading for another planet; his movements caused me to shoot back heavily and unexpectedly into my body with a great thump. I was badly shaken and angrily told him he'd ruined my travel plans! You can guess his reply. And in case you're wondering, I still very much enjoy these escapades.

Throughout my life so far, I have astrally travelled into many dimensions and been made aware of the countless levels that exist beyond our physical plane. It's rather like journeying to the many countries in the world and being able to observe the various 'tribes', their differing traditions and ways of living, without having any attachment to them, only a sense of their feelings, their sadnesses and their joys. It is great to 'touch base' in this way sometimes, but not to dwell too long, as what you experience can rub off on you, forming an attachment that will affect your mood adversely in your waking hours or even your own progression.

The misty people

In my early twenties, I used to go home most weekends, and it was during these times that I enjoyed the most amazing night visions. As soon as I had turned the light out, I would often become aware that there were a number of spirit people in my room. What seemed strange to me was the fact that I was still fully awake at the time, sitting up in bed with my eyes open.

Yet here they were, all busy working away around me, even if I couldn't make out what they were doing. They never had any colour or sharp definition (which is why I call them the misty people), but I could see well enough that there were five of them. I could follow their outlines, glimpse their clothing and tell who was male and who female. It was like watching a silent movie in 3D, but if I lost concentration or got too tired I lost the picture.

I found the whole experience truly intriguing, and when my twin stayed in my room and couldn't see anything, I was really upset. I would give her a running commentary as to what was happening.

After I had been observing these delightful goings-on for some months, one of the 'ladies' turned to me, without any physical expression or verbal communication, and handed me a platter with a large bunch of grapes on it. I was staggered to be so personally involved and found myself smiling warmly back and silently accepting the gift. For some reason, it seemed inappropriate to speak to these people, perhaps because they never spoke to me. It just seemed wrong to do so. After that, I never saw them again.

Months later, while I was visiting Doris (the medium who taught me so much), she quite suddenly stopped and mentioned these same spirit people. It was always a shock when she did things like that, as I never divulged my experiences to anyone but my twin, so it was a bit like realising that all my innermost thoughts and secrets were being aired around the universe! Very seriously, Doris told me that I had been handed the 'fruits of life'. At first I didn't quite follow, but then she said, 'The bowl of grapes – you know the one.' Then it all flooded back in my mind with a big WOW!

In my psychic journeyings, I have seen the good, the bad and the ugly – each to their own is my philosophy. I can only tell you of my discoveries, my learning and my experiences. You in turn should be assured that you have that 'knowing' already buried within you. When you find it, when you are ready to see, you will know if it feels right and is true. Once found, nobody can take that knowing away from you.

So, with my spirit colleagues and teachers as my very closest mentors and friends, I have been learning my spiritual lessons steadily and continuously throughout my life, and the day that all that stops is the day I won't need to be here any more!

CAN SPIRITS COMMUNICATE IN ANY WAY OTHER THAN VIA A PSYCHIC?

The answer to that question is, oh yes! Moving objects and using the telephone are perfect examples, although the phone messages are usually short. There have been several recorded instances of messages being received on a computer without connection to the internet, although I believe this method of interfacing to be still in an early stage of development for those on the other side as well as for us. It is interesting to note that airwaves cross the divide between worlds, so when science has enabled us to tune into higher, faster frequencies, we will all be able to go to 'spirit communication centres' and make contact with the other side in a very similar way to going to an internet cafe. I am certain there will be contact this way soon, but not just yet.

When spirit people start moving objects about in your home, they are trying to let you know they're around. It is their way of getting your attention. I have often passed on the message to a client that a loved one keeps moving a specific item in their homes. Very often the response has been, 'I knew that was happening, but I thought I was going mad and didn't like to say anything.'

In my experience, when spirit people communicate via the phone it rings with a slightly distorted ring – it's certainly not the tone you are used to hearing normally. Then, when you put the phone to your ear, just for a second or two there is what I can only describe as a strange sense of a huge void, rather like the sounds you get when you receive a long distance call with a bad connection. The voice you hear is likely to be that of someone who you were very close to and who has already passed over. It catches you at a time when you least expect it, so much so that for an instant you take it for granted that the person is there, only to be greatly disappointed when the line quickly cuts off.

One day, I found myself telling my mother-in-law, Dorothy, about phone calls from the dead. To my surprise, looking almost ashamed, she told me that she had received such a call a few years earlier. She hadn't dared tell anyone before. She was passing the phone in the hall at home when it rang. She answered it in her usual way with a 'Hello' and heard a bright, 'It's your Mum here, Dorothy. How are you?' She was in no doubt whatsoever that it was her own mother speaking. Her voice was as clear as crystal, just as if she was calling from next door. Then, just as Dorothy replied with an astonished, 'Mum, is that really you?', the phone went dead.

WAKE-UP CALL: **YOUR PSYCHIC EXPERIENCES**

- Now give yourself time to sit down and carefully consider what psychic experiences you might have had to date. Think about anything you might have discounted as 'mad' or some kind of trick.

- Now fill in the following chart, which has been created to help you remember anything significant that has happened to you.

 PERSONAL PSYCHIC EXPERIENCES

Put a tick on the dotted line after each statement that applies to you.

1. I knew who was calling before I picked up the phone. ....

2. I was just thinking about a particular person when I bumped into them (or they called me). ....

3. I was listening to a conversation and I knew what was going to happen next. ....

4. I had a dream about someone I hadn't seen for ages, then they rang me the next day. ....

5. I was looking through my phone book when I fixed on a name for a moment, then that person contacted me the same day. ....

6. I visited a place that made me feel very uneasy
    and sick.   ------------------

7. I often sense a presence around me at home.   ------------------

8. I get drawn to buy certain old objects in antique
    shops.   ------------------

9. I sometimes get an impulse to phone my family
    and then I find out something has just happened
    that they needed to tell me.   ------------------

10. I bought a present for a friend or family member
    at Christmas and it was exactly the same present
    they had bought me.   ------------------

If you got 9–10 ticks   Brilliant, you are a sensitive, this book will
                               help you understand why and how you are
                               picking up so much.

If you got 6–8 ticks   Very good. Doing this training will teach you
                               to trust and translate your feelings.

If you got 1–5 ticks   Great, you are sensing, so don't dismiss
                               it. This training will give you the full
                               knowledge you need to have confidence
                               with the work.

If you got no ticks   OK, once you have followed the
                               'wake-up calls' in this book you will have
                               opened up the doorway to your innate
                               psychic ability.

GET PHYSICAL 3
AND GO BEYOND

Now back to the real business. In Chapter One, I invited you to give yourself a 'psychic takeaway' (see page 34). You should get yourself into a happy positive state by giving yourself one of these inspirational moments each and every time you get ready to do psychic work. You are on an exciting journey after all. That feeling of excitement will actually stimulate a healthy increase in dopamine in your brain – rather like getting a happy fix!

BALANCING THE SENSES

Having got yourself into the right frame of mind, the first practical thing you need to do is balance your physical senses. The simple exercise on page 60 will not only aid your physical body to clear any blocks but also act as a loud wake-up call for your dormant psychic powers. As you work each of the physical senses one by one, and then in unison, you will be naturally trip-switching the subtle senses that exist beyond the physical level.

The first of these subtle senses is the sixth sense. Most people know this as intuition, which for most of us is a hit-and-miss affair, depending on our mood and the situation we are in at the time. However, there are also seventh, eighth and ninth senses, which will also be kick-started by these exercises.

Please remember however, that no matter how advanced you are in your psychic development, time and time again you will need to go back to basics in order to re-align yourself. We all do. Stress, anger, upset and illness can all subdue or fog the power that has been activated. Please also remember that once fully activated this power must be used fully, even in your normal everyday life. It is rather like keeping a car running and regularly serviced. The following chapters will show you various fun ways of working so that you can do just that.

First a brief word on the five physical senses.

The physical senses

Of the five physical senses, three are known as the primary ones. These are sight, hearing and touch, and they are the three senses we humans most rely on. The majority of us are predisposed to use one more than any other in our everyday lives. You can easily tell which sense a person most gravitates towards by listening to their conversation. For example:

- 'I don't see that.' (Sight)
- 'I hear what you say.' (Hearing)
- 'I don't feel right with what you're saying.' (Touch)

In order to be able to converse with people successfully, be it for business or pleasure, it is important to be able to recognise and work with that person's own primary sense. In other words, to communicate optimally with a 'sight' person, you would need to use written material and pictures to get their full attention and understanding. A 'hearer' would prefer to listen to the actual words you speak, while a 'touch' person would actually need to be touched before you could successfully talk to them.

The other two physical senses, smell and taste, can also be identified in conversation. For example:

- 'I don't like that smell, it reminds me of something in my childhood I didn't like.' (Smell)

- 'That's not my cup of tea.' (Taste)

The psychic senses

For a psychic the physical senses have extra dimensions. I describe them in the following way:

1. **Sight** 'Seeing' beyond normal human vision. Seeing outside yourself is 'outer' vision; seeing within your head is 'inner' vision.

2. **Hearing** Picking up impulses, sounds, noises or voices beyond normal hearing that others cannot. Hearing outside the head it is 'outer' hearing. If you are right-handed, the left ear picks up negative communications (ghost people) and the right picks up positive communications (spirit people); it's the other way round if you are left-handed. Getting prompts inside the head is 'inner' hearing.

3. **Touch** Feeling or sensing beyond physical touch (clairsentience) and translating energy from objects (psychometry). A feeling passes through the finger pads and impresses detailed thought forms in your consciousness, which are then expressed as images, thoughts or emotions. With practice you can also learn to identify male and female energies in this way.

4. **Smell** Picking up smells that others are not aware of and which appertain to spirit communication. Examples might be a perfume or a pungent stench, which will relate to a smell associated personally with the spirit.

5. **Taste** Getting a strange taste in the mouth or having a glass of water turn acidic due to a spirit endeavouring to communicate a message. As with smell, the taste will relate to a food or drink associated with the spirit personally.

As I have already mentioned, beyond the first five senses with which we are generally familiar, sensitives are aware of four more. These are as follows:

6. **Intuition** A sudden sense of what is going to happen; a feeling; an inner vision or hearing; or a knowing who is about to telephone When a sensitive is in a relaxed or day-dreaming state, intuition can come into play quite naturally.

7. **Clairvoyance** Seeing with 'inner' and 'outer' vision, with the use of an active pituitary gland. The sensitive has become more readily able to enter a relaxed state, in tune with the Earth's frequency (7.83 hertz), allowing visual images to come about both mentally (inner) and remotely (outer). This is explained in more detail in Chapter Five.

8. **Clairaudience** Hearing with 'inner' and 'outer' hearing, with the use of an active pineal gland. Again, the sensitive has become more readily able to enter a relaxed

state, allowing prompts of inner hearing (as in telepathy) as well as the hearing of sounds and voices remotely, outside the head.

9. **Mediumship** Activation of the third eye, through exercise. The pineal and pituitary gland both work in unison, so creating a molecular motion of 'brain-sand', which in turn activates magnetic filings that exist in the bone between the eyes (believed to lie dormant in most people today). The person who has activated this ninth sense – be they a psychic, a medium or a shaman – is considered to be an adept and can receive messages through vision, hearing, touch, smell and taste.

Once one has opened up these pathways and become an adept, it is inevitable that seeing and hearing beyond that which is known to be normal can and will occur at any time or place when you are relaxed or day-dreaming unless it is controlled.

You should also be aware that the energy field of an adept is like a working, glowing transmitter and it will be sensed instinctively by animals and some other humans in their vicinity. Like the beacon it is, it will also attract spirits, ghosts and entities, so watch out and make sure you protect yourself in the ways explained in this book!

WAKE-UP CALL: **GETTING INTO BALANCE**

Now for the simple exercise to get you into balance. So book yourself a quiet half-hour, turn off all your phones and make sure you are not going to be disturbed. The idea is to get your physical senses working properly, one by one. Then they can begin to work in a balanced way in unison. The exercise is also fun to do with friends.

You will need: A blindfold, a note pad and pen, a sprig of mint and a sprig of thyme (or any other herb except sage – the smell is too strong), a small glass of tap water (label the underside of the glass 'No 1'), a small glass of tonic water (label the underside of the glass 'No 2'), a small glass of bottled water (label the underside of the glass 'No 3'), four or five small items from around your home (eg a crystal, a piece of jewellery, a tiny box) in a carrier bag, a copy of the progress sheet on page 62.

- Sit on a comfortable chair or sofa, with all the above items in front of you on a table.

- Put on the blindfold, then swap the glasses of water around so you don't know which is which. (Take care handling the glasses with the blindfold on.) Take the blindfold off again. You are now ready to start balancing.

- Sit peacefully for a moment. Take a breath in and then out. Do this three times, then smile.

- Start with your first sense, sight. Tell yourself that you are going to look at everything around you in the room, and then, remaining seated, do so. Take in the shapes, the colours, what pleases and what displeases you. Do this for two minutes, then stop and take a breath.

- Commit all you have seen to memory. Do not make any notes yet.

- Put on the blindfold. (Keep it on until the very end of the exercise.)

- Now move on to your second sense, hearing. Tell yourself you are going to hear and absorb every sound. Do this for two minutes, then stop and take a breath.

- Memorise all you have heard. Do not write any notes yet.

- Now move on to your third sense, touch. Tell yourself you are going to feel (and feel only) all of the items in the carrier bag. Do so, absorbing the touch sensations, comfortable or uncomfortable, hard or soft, sharp or dull. You may also get flashes of colour. Do this for three minutes, then stop, take a breath and shake your hands.

- Memorise your touch sensations. Do not make any notes yet.

- Now move on to your fourth sense, smell. Tell yourself you are going to smell (and smell only) each of the herbs. Pick the first one up, rub it between your fingers and put it to your nose. Take in the scent for a few seconds and then put it down. Do the same with the other herb. You may find they trip-switch old memories, happy or sad; you may like or dislike the scents. Do this for two minutes then stop, take a breath and rub your hands.

- Memorise the smells and their effects. Do not make any notes yet.

- Now move on to your fourth sense, taste. Take a sip of the water in one of the three. Give the taste some thought. Did you like or dislike it? Do the same with each of the other two glasses. When you have finished, stop, take a breath and spend a few moments relaxing.

- Memorise the tastes. Do not take any notes yet.

- Take off the blindfold and write down your responses to each of the five tests in your note pad, summarising them on the progress sheet. Only when you have finished writing should you read on from here.

PROGRESS SHEET

So what did you pick up?   **Marks**

SIGHT

How many colours did you notice?

If 1	+ 1	....
2 or more	+ 4	....

How many shapes did you notice?

If 1	+ 1	....
2 or more	+ 4	....

Did you look at different textures?

If yes	+ 1	....

Did you have likes or dislikes?

If yes	+ 1	....

(Maximum score 10 points)   SCORE: ....

HEARING

How many sounds did you hear?

If 1	+ 1	....
2–4	+ 5	....
5 plus	+ 6	....

Did you get silence after a moment?

If yes	+ 4	....

(Maximum score 10 points)   SCORE: ....

TOUCH

Did you feel the shape of each object?

If yes	+ 2	....

Did you get a flash of colour?

1–2 colours	+ 4	....
3–5 colours	+ 5	....

Did you like the feel of the objects?

1–3 objects	+ 2	....
4–5 objects	+ 3	....

Did you get no sense of feeling?   Nil   ....

(Maximum score 10 points)   SCORE: ....

SMELL

Did you enjoy both smells?

If yes	+ 5	....

Did you get a pleasant memory?

1 or more	+ 4	....

Did you get an unpleasant memory?

1 or more	+ 1	....

(Maximum score 10 points)   SCORE: ....

TASTE

Did you get a taste from all three glasses of water?

If yes	+ 4	....
1–2	+ 2	....

Did a taste give you a good memory?

1–2	+ 2	....

Did you like only one taste?

Yes	+ 2	....

Did you dislike any of the tastes?

1–2	+ 2	....
3	+ 1	....
Did you get nothing?	Nil	....
(Maximum score 10 points)	SCORE:	....

SUMMARY OF SCORES

Sight	....
Hearing	....
Touch	....
Smell	....
Taste	....
(Maximum score 50)	TOTAL: ....

Now let's look at your score. Relax – there are no good or bad answers. It's not a competition. However, what you have memorised and written down will indicate your degree of sensitivity on a scale of one to ten. More importantly, it will tell you whether you are better suited to being a clairvoyant, a clairaudient or a clairsentient. Training in each of these areas can give you great psychic ability. If you find that you are equally perceptive with all the senses, you may already be well on the way to becoming an adept.

If you scored 48–50   Very impressive! You are a true sensitive with excellent awareness, and you naturally use your ability in everyday life. Your physical senses are working in balance and you are already using the sixth, seventh, eighth and ninth senses to some degree. By the end of the training you should be using your psychic power with ever greater knowledge and accuracy.

If you scored 40–47   Excellent. You are clearly ready to move on to the next step in developing psychic awareness. However, if you ever falter or feel blocked in any way, go back and re-balance your senses again.

If you scored 30–40   Good. You can go forward to the next step, but if you do not manage Chapter Four successfully the first time round, then you will need to go back and re-balance your senses again, after which you should find you will command a much better response.

If you scored 20–30   Average. You need to balance your senses again – but this time you should find it much easier and your score will naturally improve. Then you will be ready to proceed to Chapter Four.

If you scored 4–19   Your physical senses are blocked and out of balance. Do this 'wake-up call' again and see how your score changes. If you achieve 30 or more, try moving on to the next chapter. If your score is still below 30, you will need to do the 'wake-up call' a third time to improve your results.

Some may have more work to do than others, but remember, the greater the work, the greater the achievement! It does take energy and effort to do the training, at every stage. I have found that to do something well requires a belief in oneself and the knowledge that there are no boundaries, so if you are truly convinced that you can be the best, you will be.

CODE A AND THE BASIC PROTOCOLS

I use the term Code A to represent the perfect brain frequency for all psychic and spiritual work. There are three basic protocols for achieving it. Once you are familiar with them, it will eventually take only a few seconds to cut in to the frequency and work. Understand that *you* are in charge of your body and your mind, and *you* will be creating the time and space to do the work when you are ready.

Try out the basic protocols now, as you will be using them at the start of each wake-up call that follows.

The basic protocols

1. Alter your mood to a positive and happy state.

2. Make sure all phones, computers, TVs, CD players and so on are switched off and that there will be no interruptions. Sit in an upright position on a chair with both feet on the ground, legs uncrossed. Relax your shoulders and hands.

3. Take three easy breaths in and out. Feel the muscles relax throughout your body and just sit for a few minutes with your eyes closed.

How do you know you are in Code A?

Believe it or not, you already find yourself in Code A quite naturally every day of your life. It is the brain frequency you enter during those moments when you find yourself day-dreaming, or quietly doing the household chores alone, or waiting at traffic lights, or simply allowing your mind to wander, perhaps as you spend a relaxing moment in the bathroom or take a peaceful walk in the countryside. So it's nothing new; it's just my terminology that may be unfamiliar.

I will be talking more about Code A in Chapter Four. Suffice it to say here that the brain quickly becomes accustomed to this shift through exercise and regular usage. You will find it happens quite naturally. Once your brain is attuned in this way, you can simply use the command 'Code A' to tune in fast and accurately.

Sensitives can read other people's thought waves, but if you want to learn how to make the most of your ability, you have also to learn how to take full control. If you can do this success-fully, you will be able to pick up on the energy fields around the living, read imprints left on inanimate objects and activate your own aerial to get messages from beyond the grave or into the future.

As I have already said, while there are as many levels, or dimensions, on the other side as there are different types of people in the world, if you follow my methods you will, through command, be safely receiving from the highest only, with integrity and good grace.

 PSYCHIC TAKEAWAY: **YOU ARE MORE THAN GOOD ENOUGH**

Stand in front of a mirror and tell yourself out loud:

- I am the power.
- I am gifted in this work.
- I am the best.

Do this morning and night each day. The chatter of your subconscious mind telling you that you are not good enough will slowly but surely cease and the new commands you are giving your mind will quickly sink in and take effect.

BE THE PERFECT 4
TELEPATH

Telepathy is the ability to transmit a message to another person (the receiver) through the mind, without using speech, writing, touch or any other signal. The technique I am going to share with you is 120 per cent successful. I refer not to 100 per cent because to be the best you must always be well beyond the highest norm!

Read this chapter carefully, because if you are not successful the first time around, you have let something slip. Give your work thought, as thought is the force that drives it all. Everything is conceived in the mind before coming into material or physical being. I have found that thought is like a messaging service: if you create a wish in the moment, it will gradually move into your life – but more on this later. You should also keep up a good pace. Gaps of nothingness allow the nagging chatter of the subconscious to intrude and interrupt you.

INCREASE YOUR PSYCHIC POWER WITH EXCITEMENT AND LAUGHTER

In my experience, the very best students in this work are those who enjoy moments of excitement and laughter, both of which naturally cause higher levels of dopamine to be secreted in the brain. Dopamine has been proven to be very beneficial in psychic work. If you find yourself feeling down or miserable, give your-

. do the relaxation and self-healing 'psychic take-
. 71. This will give you a wonderful feeling of calm,
.se levels of serotonin beneficially, as well as greatly
aidi... ...u in terms of decreasing worry and lowering stress. If
you are currently in pain or suffering from an ailment, it is bound
to pull you down as well as lowering your immune system. In
this case, I would suggest that you do the relaxation and self-
healing exercise daily until you feel your old self again. You
should then create an inspirational moment by repeating the
'psychic takeaway' exercise on page 34. This will create a great
boost before you send out a psychic message.

I'm a great believer in laughter. It has benefits for your whole
being, resonating positively in your body rather like a perfectly
pitched musical note. It has also been scientifically proven that
eating some chocolate raises the immune system in minutes –
although I for one don't need any excuse for eating chocolate.

Another tip is to watch a comedy show or a funny film. This
really will alter your mood advantageously. Have you noticed just
how you feel after watching a sad film or seeing angry people
shouting on TV? I'm not saying you should never watch such
things; just be aware of the effect they have on your whole being.
All sounds resonate positively or negatively with every life form,
In the same vein, words have great power. I make it a rule not to
allow students to use words that pop out on 'automatic mode'
(i.e. coming from the subconscious), so creating interference
during psychic work. Have a look at the following examples:

NO – your subconscious is talking	YES – sensitive speak
I think . . .	I feel . . .
My gut tells me . . .	I sense . . .
I follow my nose.	I pick up.

When you speak, try to be conscious of the words you are using and what they really mean. That way, you will be ensuring that your psychic power does not drain away unnecessarily.

 PSYCHIC TAKEAWAY: RELAXATION AND SELF-HEALING

This exercise is greatly beneficial. You should do it at least once a week, as well as whenever you are feeling tired or stressed. You can do it alone or with a group of friends. Once you have learnt the exercise, you can keep your eyes closed all the way through and enjoy.

- Find a quiet place. Sit upright in a comfortable chair, with your legs uncrossed. Relax your shoulders.

- Take three breaths in and out. Feel your shoulders drop back. Take another breath in and out – relax. Now read the following out loud:
  - I am calling on the spirit net to draw the most powerful fluid of bright white light into this room. It is coming in and increasing over my head and is flowing around my head in a positive motion. It is increasing in volume as I speak.
  - This beautiful source of energy is now flowing down through the top of my head. As it does so, it is going to increase my well-being, re-energise me, clear any blocks in my system, wash away any negativity, and leave me feeling fully revitalised and refreshed.

- Now imagine the white fluid sealing over the head region and allow the rest to swirl away exactly as it arrived. If your eyes are closed, you can open them.

- Just sit for a few minutes and enjoy the feeling of bliss within. You are fully relaxed, at peace and any chatter should now have ceased in your head.

WAKE-UP CALL: **THE PHONE CALL**

Having relaxed and healed yourself by giving yourself the 'psychic take-away' on page 71, it is now the perfect time to work on a telepathic transmission. In this exercise you will be sending a psychic message to someone. When doing any mind work such as this, always remember to keep everything precise and simple. The key to the exercise is creating shape, colour and movement in your visualisation. The moment this happens, the recipient will receive a strong prompt from you, rather like a radio wave giving them a blast in the head! Later they will tell you, 'I suddenly started thinking about you', 'I couldn't get you out of my head', 'I got a sudden picture of you in my mind and felt I had to contact you', or even 'You've been on my mind for days, so I thought I'd better get in touch'.

Some people will naturally try to fight this impulse (I think it's a man thing especially). Reason and logic can stop us doing the best of things, and no one wants to risk making themselves look silly by contacting someone for no reason. In particular, if you try this exercise with an ex-boyfriend or girlfriend who has been avoiding you since your break-up, you should be aware that they may go out of their way to block any thoughts whatsoever that come into their head connected with you – as you probably would too in the same circumstances. In general, though, the more the recipient of your message tries to resist it, the more it will nag them mentally to make contact.

Never try to send more than one message at a time, and at first do only one a day. Practise on a variety of people over the days and weeks to build up confidence in your ability and gain your own evidence that psychic messaging really works. After a while, the phone company will probably notice that you've reduced your calls!

- Find a quiet place where you will not be disturbed. Sit upright in a comfortable chair, with your legs uncrossed. Relax your shoulders.

- Create an inspirational moment by giving yourself the 'psychic take-away' on page 34.

- Decide on one individual to send your message to. Choose someone who knows and likes you, and with whom you have a rapport.

- Close your eyes and take three breaths in and out.

- Create in your mind a glistening, golden-white line in the shape figure eight across your forehead, starting on the right-hand side. It is like a racing circuit. If you cannot imagine it, tell yourself that it is there.

- Move around the figure eight several times with no breaks, keeping your thought in line with the movement.

- Now make the figure eight into a single windscreen wiper, moving back and forth across your forehead within a golden-white light.

- Take a breath, then imagine that there is a large cinema screen in front of you, with a bright blue surround. Onto the right-hand side of the screen project a bright-red telephone. Again, if you cannot imagine it, just tell yourself that it is there. Onto the left-hand side, project the person you are sending the message to – in colour.

- Smiling, say firmly and positively, '. . . . . . [first name of the person], telephone me.' Repeat this once and then say '. . . . . . [first name of the person], telephone . . . . . . [your own name].' As you speak these sentences, move the person to the telephone and see them press the keypad to dial your number.

- Smile, take a breath and imagine a white light over the whole scene, then wipe away the screen in your mind and smile. It is done. Make a note of the time you transmitted.

- Now mark up the progress sheet on page 75.

Transmitters are also great receivers, so you will soon be picking up who's going to email, text or phone you before they do. This technique is now part of your daily life – don't forget that. It isn't just a plaything for a week or two. You have opened up the power and the more you allow it, work with it and enjoy it in your life, the greater the benefits will be. If anything goes wrong and the technique doesn't work, go back to basics and work through this 'wake-up call' again, making sure you have carried out all the steps as instructed.

PROGRESS SHEET

Transmission to (name)	Date	Time	Response date	Time
1.	....	....	....	....
2.	....	....	....	....
3.	....	....	....	....
4.	....	....	....	....
5.	....	....	....	....
6.	....	....	....	....
7.	....	....	....	....
8.	....	....	....	....
9.	....	....	....	....
10.	....	....	....	....

Now let's look at how you did.

All or most successful Congratulations. You've got it. Now put your new skill into practice once a day for a week or two before letting it loose as and when you need it. Notice the differences this makes in your life.

Some successes You are developing your skills. Try contacting the people you transmitted to unsuccessfully and find out if they got the prompt but blocked you. If it turns out that some of them blocked you, try again, choosing people who are more open to receiving your messages or are less busy.

All or mostly unsuccessful Make sure you are paying attention to the basics, then give it some thought and choose people who connect better with you and try again.

...OTECTION WHILE WORKING ...ALLY?

...to this question is yes. The more energy you create for y...self, the more you will be noticed by others (both in this world and beyond), so you need to be able to contain and control it. (You will find information on how to protect yourself on page 33.) Thankfully, as you will learn, there is an endless source of energy out there for you to plug into. As you connect with it and your power grows, you will find it translates into people telling you things like, 'You are so charismatic' and 'You really captivated your audience'.

TELEPATHY AND FEAR

As I mentioned earlier, one of the biggest blocks people suffer is fear. Let me remind you: fear is in your memory, it is part of your belief system, it is what you have learnt and what you may be holding on to, so it is literally stuck on the 'tape deck' in your subconscious. In order to overcome fear, you first need to under-stand where it came from. Who told you? What were you told? Then you need to ask yourself why you allow such received fears to continue in your life. Be warned that if fear is fed, especially amongst a group or crowd of people, it can easily turn to anger and aggression.

WAKE-UP CALL: **WORDS OF POWER**

You may have internalised such fear-generating messages as:

- You're stupid.
- You'll never make it in life.
- You're just not good enough.

If this is the case, now is the moment to drop it and stop it. . . Try bringing the following words into your daily life. They will help build up your self-esteem and self-belief. These are the words:

- I am the power.
- I am the light.
- I love myself.
- I am safe.

Say the words out loud to yourself with your eyes open and looking upwards first thing every morning and last thing each night before bed. Do this for two weeks. Your fears will reduce and dissipate as your self-esteem grows. And as you work through the exercises in this book, the growing evidence of your power will take you the rest of the way.

PETER'S STORY: PERSISTENCE PAYS OFF

Peter was 18 years old. He had a healthy enquiring mind, charm, sensitivity and a great sense of humour. His father had promised to pay for Peter to have a gap year abroad if he achieved the exam grades necessary for acceptance onto the psychology course he had chosen at a top university. Unfortunately, he failed to make the grades. Now he felt lost and desperately ashamed. It was at this point that Peter's parents pushed him through my door, desperately hoping that I could help him after all their efforts had failed.

Peter and I talked things through. I don't like to consider age as a deciding factor in learning; I prefer to think of the stage a person is at. So far, most of Peter's learning had been from school, but thankfully he was still at an open and receptive stage. To my mind he was very creative and outgoing, and he was well used to speaking to people socially without support from others, which was to be a great asset when working with him. I do not believe this came from his upbringing, but from an underlying knowledge of what he had learnt in previous lives. He also had what I would call an open mind – the ability to take on board a 'how to do it' key and use it for himself – so he accepted my enthusiasm for him and his future as if it was his written path.

Eventually, we came up with a plan, which Peter had the will and the energy to put into action. He truly believed in his dream and was prepared to follow it through against all the odds. I arranged a meeting for him with a group of psychologists I knew. Then, on his own, Peter made an appointment with the university that had rejected him. Face to face, he told them of his great love and passion for psychology and his desire to fulfil his dream. It worked. He got his gap year and his coveted university place. He got his degree and later went on to practise parapsychology in the USA.

Peter was someone who not only had a grasp of his life's work but was also able to begin changing his negative ways of thinking after his very first visit to me. He fully embraced the power of thinking creatively in the moment and set about earnestly cultivating belief in himself and in his ability to make things happen. I'm not saying that this was a picnic for him, but he was open and non-judgemental. He visualised and created what he desired, to the extent that I had only to give him an idea of his own potential and self-worth for him to set about organising how it was going to happen. As I said to him at the time:

> What have you got to lose? From your present standpoint you've got everything to gain, so *go* for it! Make all your phone calls in a strong and positive manner and you will shock yourself with the positive responses you get.

 WAKE-UP CALL: **BRINGING THINGS IN . . .**

This is another fun way to get your self-belief going full-time and provide yourself with evidence that your telepathic abilities genuinely are real before you move on to bigger, greater ideas.

- Give yourself an inspirational moment by doing the 'psychic takeaway' on page 34.
- Follow the steps for the telephone 'wake-up call' on page 72, but instead of a phone and a friend, visualise the person (not someone you know) coming to your door with a box of chocolates.
- See yourself opening the door and the person handing you the chocolates. You take them and say a big 'Yes, thank you!'

This exercise really works, but you must keep it this simple and really mean it. Remember, the universe is all yours and does not judge you. You can also do this exercise with a bunch of flowers.

WAKE-UP CALL: . . . **AND SENDING THEM AWAY**

If you can draw all you wish for into your life, then the opposite must also apply: you can also block things that you do not want in order to safeguard yourself. Let's say, for example, you're meant to meet someone today – it could be a business contact, a family member or a friend – but you truly don't want to see them. As usual, you don't know how to get out of it. Well, here's your solution! I must point out that you should never do this exercise with any bad feelings or attachment to the result – both are negative and will void the whole exercise.

- Give yourself an inspirational moment by doing the 'psychic takeaway' on page 34.

- Follow the steps for the telephone 'wake-up call' on page 72, but instead of a phone and a friend, visualise green grass with a hill behind and blue sky above.

- Just for a moment, project the person you are scheduled to meet onto the screen, in colour, facing you. Then, very fast, imagine a huge gold X in front of them and push them up and over the hill – make them disappear in a second.

- Then wipe away the screen in your mind and smile. It is done.

Do not question, simply trust. This works too. And if it doesn't, you know why: you let in mental chatter that belongs to your old disbelief syndrome! In which case, start again and re-transmit the message.

A NOTE ON THE SCIENCE BEHIND TELEPATHIC TRANSMISSION

Psychic power comes with self-empowerment. It is directed from the true will of consciousness. Phrases that are connected with this will include:

- I am.
- I can.
- I do.
- I will.
- I have.
- And it shall be . . . from this moment on.

Nikolai Kozyrev, a Russian scientist, says: 'Time is a form of energy. It is to time's properties that we should look in order to find the source that maintains the phenomenon of life in the world.' According to Kozyrev, telepathy and ESP (extra-sensory perception) are both forms of time energy that appear immediately everywhere! Telepathy creates an energy that is denser near the receiver of an action and thinner near the sender. This has been fully tested with gyroscopes, asymmetrical pendulums and torsion balancers (the pendulum is made with a gyroscope). So, in short, time is thin around the cause and dense around the effect.

However, time density can be affected by changes in the weather – such as thunderstorms – and in the season. In the far north, where everything is covered by snow and there are fewer living things, telepathy flows more easily. Gravity also has an effect on time density, as does the density of matter.

There is certainly truth in old sayings such as 'Practice

makes perfect' and 'Where there's a will, there's a way'. I can't resist adding, 'A strong desire to achieve drives the energy through to create your goal'.

PSYCHIC POWER AND MIND-ALTERING SUBSTANCES

I believe that taking any substance at all that weakens the ability of the conscious mind to maintain control will lessen the potential for spiritual or psychic development.

Anyone who has been down the road of substance abuse, be the substance alcohol or drugs, will know that it does seriously dull the mind, creating a numbness and an inability to take or maintain control of the will. Any substance that has this effect is to me truly mind-altering, and if you need to use – or choose to continue using – such substances, I would strongly advise you not to follow the path of psychic development any further.

I am aware that a lot has been written recently on the taking of psychotropic drugs by spiritual adepts, such as shamans, in the past. However, I firmly believe it to be extremely dangerous for anyone to do this who has not first gone through advanced spiritual training in order to control the power that such substances can unleash. It is possible to literally lose yourself, your mind and your soul if you have not done so first. You may also gravely damage the protective outer layer around the physical body, known as the subtle body or the etheric layer, in particular around the head area. This will leave you open to attack from highly unpleasant entities, which may attach themselves to you. The outward signs of such attack may be sudden mood-swings; sudden, sometimes violent aggression; hearing voices (in the left ear) and worse.

THE PHYSICAL, ETHERIC AND ASTRAL BODIES

The diagram below illustrates the three layers of the body, the physical, the etheric and the astral. The etheric is a subtle body and therefore cannot be seen with the naked eye. It generally extends some 7.5 cm (3 in) outside the physical body, although it can expand to as much as 1 m (3 ft) when you are mixing with friends, feeling happy and safe. However, if you direct your attention to the use of the etheric layer as an energy field, then you can extend it at will. As part of their training, some adepts actually throw a part of this field towards others and cause them to fall down when they are least expecting it! The etheric layer bears the scars of any and every invasive attack on the body – for example surgery, accidents, and all other wounds experienced during one's lifetime (all of which can be read by a trained psychic).

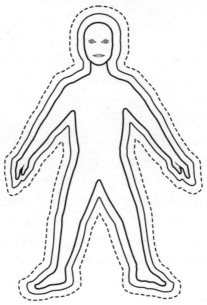

Beyond the etheric body lies the astral body, generally unnoticed. While you are awake, it is in what I would term a dormant state, but when you are sleeping it can literally slip away, remaining attached to the navel by a silvery elastic cord, which allows it to travel incredible distances. Astral travel can be led by your soul's intention or – with practice – by conscious thought. Every living human travels during sleep at some time or another, although they are usually unconscious of the experience taking place. Some people will wake up remembering they have been floating or flying, but the memory is usually jumbled up within a subconscious dream. When you are very tired or stressed and suddenly fall asleep, you often wake up with a start, as if you were falling. That is your astral body being jolted back into your physical body.

THE LEFT AND RIGHT BRAIN

The diagram on page 85 shows the uses of the left and right brain. Be aware that if you are left-handed, the uses of the two brain lobes will be the other way around.

Left brain: The subconscious

The subconscious brain is rather like a tape deck that runs on automatic most of the time. Inter-communicating tapes cover all the necessary areas to run your body functions. It is from the subconscious mind that mental chatter comes. However, this mental chatter can be controlled by way of commands or affirmations. With determined effort, you will find that the chatter decreases, eventually to the extent that you will be able to say no to any emotion or rationale that may interfere with your psychic work.

Right brain: The conscious

It is in the right brain that true psychic power lies. You can develop this power quite simply by using considered commands that are an expression of your true will. According to my own definition, true will is the ability to act or refrain from acting at any one time. This is where you can purposefully create 'sensitive speak'.

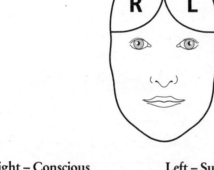

Right – Conscious	Left – Subconscious
Used for accessing your soul/ higher self	Holds memories good/bad of all you hear, see, touch and taste
Communication from spirit	Memories of past life traumas
Receiving and transmitting thought waves	Instinctive reactions of fear
Intuitive sensing	Automatic responses and reactions
Creative imagination in vision, thought and sense of feeling	Emotions
Work with the third eye	Memory bank of all learning *Fantasies and dreams* *Sexual responses* *Doubts and worries*

Review: what have you achieved so far?

Since we're nearing the halfway stage, let's take a moment to reflect on what you have learnt so far.

- You have balanced your five physical senses and begun to activate the sixth, seventh, eighth and ninth senses.

- You are giving your mind and body a boost by doing the inspirational moment 'psychic takeaway' daily (see page 34).

- You are using the relaxation and self-healing 'psychic takeaway' daily or weekly (see page 71).

- You have begun to develop your telepathic ability by learning how to transmit simple messages to friends and family anywhere.

- You have learnt to call fun things into your everyday life without leaving home!

- You have learnt how to cancel a meeting psychically.

- You know that you are more than just a physical body and have an understanding of the way in which the etheric body protects you.

- You have an understanding of the role of left and right brain, and are beginning to be able to take control of your mind at will.

Having mastered all this, congratulate yourself. You will love the next chapter.

VOICES IN YOUR HEAD 5

Clearing the chatter in your head is difficult, I know, but the sound of silence is what you are after. When you finally achieve it, it will allow your psychic messages to come through loud and clear. The brain frequency chart on page 89 will tell you which brainwave you are generally running on in your everyday life. In this chapter you will be learning how to tune into the appropriate brainwaves to enable you to do your psychic work.

BRAIN FREQUENCIES AND CODE A

As we have already noted (see page 66) Code A – 7.83 hertz, the Earth's own rhythm – is the ideal frequency for psychic work. All earthly life forms – animals, plants, fish, insects and so on – connect to and utilise this frequency, and we humans, too, were once naturally attuned to it in all that we did, resonating intuitively with the rhythms and movements of the other life forms and instinctively aware of what was going on around us and why. As a result of our subsequent evolution, most of us have lost most if not all of this ability to tune into Code A (having found, it seems, other more selfish and material ways to control our environment). However, traces of this ability remain, lying dormant deep down in all of us, and in some much closer to the surface.

A true adept has the ability to tune in and out of this most fundamental of frequencies and do their work instinctively. I am sure you yourself can think of world-renowned spiritual leaders, Buddhist monks, shamans, mediums and true healers who are able to do this quite naturally, setting emotions and rationalisations aside in order to receive wisdom and pass on deep truths. In the distant past, it was much easier for sensitives to do this, as by and large they would have lived in peaceful, remote places, untouched by the stresses most people have to live with today.

Watching, talking to and listening to other psychics as I often do, it seems to me that many do not fully understand quite how, why or from where psychic communication comes about, preferring instead to say, 'It just happens', or to call it a gift brought on by chance or an accident. In fact, psychism is a primitive ability naturally open to all. It is as if we all have a psychic chip lodged deep within our brains just waiting to be re-activated.

In my experience, the information and exercises contained within this book will without a doubt re-activate this chip. They will train you to relax, to quiet the chatter of your everyday mind and achieve Code A at will. Once learnt, these techniques will ensure that on command your brain slips naturally and easily into this state, whenever you wish it and wherever you are. So persevere. It really is worth it.

Our brain frequency is naturally affected by subconscious interruptions, such as worry or excessive thinking, as well as by noise and hustle and bustle around us. The reason meditation has become so popular is that it helps people to relax enough to quiet, or still, the subconscious and allow pure consciousness through instead. I personally do not agree with the idea that meditation is about creating a gap or a void in consciousness. In my opinion, unless you hold a command or affirmation in your mind, the void that results will allow mental chatter to slip back in.

The relaxation techniques and protocols in this book naturally log you onto Code A. However, you may find yourself

Brain frequencies

Gamma – over 35 hertz
Used only when peak performance – i.e.
a high degree of mental and physical
accuracy – is required, for example a pilot
landing a plane or a tennis pro engaged
in a rapid-fire volley. (The Gamma state
has only recently been defined.)

Beta – 13–35 hertz
Used in states of active or focused
consciousness, such as reading this book.
Also found in states of anxiety and stress.
The normal active frequency for many
people.

Alpha – 8–12.5 hertz
Used in states of unstressed, directed
attention. An efficient waking state,
found just after waking.

Code A – 7.83 hertz*
The perfect brain rhythm for psychism,
creating a still space in which information
can be transmitted/received, and past,
present or future events can be viewed.
(This is also the rhythm of the Earth and
is known as 'the cosmic clock'.)

Theta – 4–7 hertz
Predominant in the dream state and in deep
meditation. Can be used for trance work.

Delta – 1–3 hertz
A deep sleep state

Note: At around 12 years of age a child's EEG spectrum begins to show sustained
periods of an even higher frequency, defined as Beta waves of 13–35 hertz.

*While the other brain rhythms described in this table are accepted by scientists, I have
added Code A because I am convinced it is the only brainwave that enables us to do
psychic work properly and successfully.

slipping into a deeper state of Theta. You will know that this has happened if you experience the kind of stillness and peace you fall into before going to sleep. This is the state used for trance work, in which you allow your consciousness to step aside and give over control to spirit. However, this is advanced work, requiring learning, practice and experience. If you do find yourself slipping into Theta, you should command yourself to pull out of this state and back into Code A.

THE SPIRIT NET

Working in Code A will make you an excellent receiver. It is rather like becoming a messenger service from the spirit net, where I believe all knowledge and information is held. Within the net are what were known in pre-Hindu India as the Akashic records – akasha means 'ether' in Sanskrit. These are the details of all human beings, animals, plants and other life forms that have lived and live now. Each has its own 'disc', which can be accessed and read by the sensitive on request, in much the same way that a computer will access and read a CD-ROM. However, the spirit world has many levels, and no sensitive, however well attuned, can expect (while alive) to obtain any more knowledge than they are capable of absorbing or understanding.

Spirit people – those who have passed over and gone back to the spirit net – have gained the freedom to choose whether they communicate directly with those they know and love who are still alive, or whether (as they often do) to pass their message on via a guide – that is, one who has chosen to work with a sensitive. (They tell me it takes as much progressive learning on their side to pass messages on as it does on ours.) Eventually, as a sensitive, you will become aware of your own guide – and in some cases more than one guide – working with you.

WAKE-UP CALL: **LISTENING WITH YOUR INNER EAR**

The idea of this exercise is to pick up subtle prompts coming from your inner hearing, deep inside your conscious mind. Before you start work, you will need to ask a number of people if you can use them as 'testers' in your new work. They should know you well enough not to be cavalier or unthinking about your psychic work but should not be close friends, about whom you will already know far too much to get a true and unbiased reading. It is better to do this exercise a few times for a short period than to try to work for too long a period at first. Going into and out of Code A regularly will quickly teach you to recognise the difference.

- Give yourself an inspirational moment (see the 'psychic takeaway' on page 34), clear your mind of background chatter and go into Code A.

- Invite your first 'tester' in. Now imagine that you have an extra ear buried in your head and start listening with it. You are looking for information such as names, numbers and words. As you get used to listening in this way, you will find that whole sentences begin to form quite naturally. The more you trust what you hear and go with the flow, the more you will receive.

- When you have finished 'listening', tune out (see page 97) and pass on whatever message you have received straightaway.

WILL I NOW BE ABLE TO RECEIVE THE WINNING LOTTERY NUMBERS?

While I would be fascinated to know what you would like to do with your win (how much would it be? . . . thousands, tens of thousands, millions . . . why stop there?), I'm afraid you cannot be attached to the outcome when you are doing psychic work.

Aside from which, projecting a limiting and limited desire only for material worth is not the point.

If and when, however, you can overcome such material limitations and learn how to use your new-found power in the most divine way, the reward can be absolute abundance, given quite freely to you to work with in your life . . . Of course, if you then shut yourself up in a vast mansion and live to excess on your massive new wealth, you will quickly be heading back down the ladder of your own progression.

That said, I do know quite a few people who have tuned in and been given three, and sometimes even four, Lottery numbers that turned out to be correct (the other numbers given were not). And I myself have had the odd good day at the races, when I seemingly couldn't put a foot wrong and every horse I picked was the winner. But I did this for amusement and with a sense of humour. It was a bit like a run on the roulette table – by the fourth race, everyone around me was backing all the horses I put my money on. But I saw it all as just a bit of fun; it wasn't the result of a desperate need to change my life.

WHY DO SOME MESSAGES I RECEIVE SEEM TOTALLY OFF BEAM?

As far as you are concerned at this stage in the learning process, nothing is what it seems. It's important to remember that the information you are given may be about past, present or future moments covering an entire lifetime. So forget the constraints of time and always tell people to remember the message.

A message that doesn't seem to be relevant at the time it is given will often prove to be significant later. Often, people need to go away and absorb what they have heard. You would be surprised how many people suddenly remember something relevant from their past later, or, on asking a friend or relative, get confirmation of what you have passed on.

I have found that when an apparently unlikely event is going to occur in someone's life, information about it is often given to them in the form of a predictive message. When the extraordinary event does indeed happen, they are excited and amazed and almost always like to give feedback to the messenger. This can be a great boost for your confidence in trusting what you get.

CHRIS'S STORY: TRAINING TO BE A STEP AHEAD

Chris was in his fifties. He had rather a formal manner and was somewhat shy – almost withdrawn. But he was charming, highly intelligent and had an intensely enquiring mind. He had trained as a nuclear physicist, then strayed into military intelligence and was now working abroad in the private sector. He was divorced with two children at college. He had a great respect and love for women but had yet to settle down a second time, something he really wanted to do.

He had a keen interest in palmistry, as well as an impressive in-depth understanding of astrology, and he had been consulting me as a medium once a year for a number of years. Each time he came for a reading, he would open his notebook and give me a regimented report on everything I had said the year before and everything that had taken place since. It always amuses me when a client does this. I never retain any memory of any information I give in a sitting. In any case, as far as I am concerned, the information is the client's, not mine. I am only the messenger.

Then, at the end of one of his annual sittings, Chris asked me if I would train him. He felt that he was at a crossroads and wanted to help himself to move forward positively and profitably in his life. He loved the idea of using the mind telepathically and of accessing all of its power and was specifically interested in becoming a seer. He felt that if he could view his future to see the business opportunities ahead, he would have the edge in making decisions about deals he was considering making. I also sensed that he wanted to attract a suitable relationship into his life.

Throughout the three years of his training, Chris was impressively studious and enthusiastic, all of which I could only applaud. However, his thoughts, centring around his burning desire to achieve results on a material level, were often too intense, verging on the point of negativity, and kept limiting his great potential. Several times I had to remind myself that this was his journey, not mine. Keeping the physical senses in good balance is vital to mastering this work, and in Chris's case balancing was something he needed to do very regularly. Thankfully, he found it easy to achieve a state of deep relaxation, and this helped him enormously.

As you would probably imagine given what I have told you about Chris, his mental commands and affirmations were all highly regimented, so to him there was never any question that he would achieve the greatest results. He was also capable of generating vast resources of energy but, depending on the fluctuations of his inner desires, he would work like a pendulum, swinging backwards and forwards between his negative and positive motives. One part of him was all about giving and intent on service to others; the other was very definitely in 'I want and will create great material worth' mode, which was why he kept faltering. He was failing to release his attachment to the outcome.

Chris spent three years training with me, steadily working through all his psychic dilemmas. and then set about enthusiastically using his new knowledge to supplement his business methods. At first he worked for some very wealthy businesses, the idea being to help them to become even wealthier, until eventually he had the funding to set up his own company – or should I say 'empire', because his business became very successful. Chris now travels the world using his extensive skills to his ever greater advantage. I believe he is a happier man – certainly his business and personal life have borne great fruit.

For myself, I often wonder who gains the most out of psychic training, me or the student, because I certainly find it a continual learning process myself and always enjoy every moment. Just when I feel sure I have at last met all the varied characters out there, I get put in my place and blown away again. There's never a chance for complacency in this work!

So never forget that this is an individual journey for each and every one of us, and we all have to work through it ourselves. Only you can seek to know your own true purpose and learn to recognise the strengths and weaknesses that will help and hinder you along the way. And for you, like everyone else, there will be hiccups or sticking points to overcome on your amazing spiritual journey.

THE PSYCHIC RULES FOR LIFE

The following psychic rules must become a natural part of your everyday life. Remember that as a messenger you can't afford to make any judgements by way of reason and logic. You should familiarise yourself with these rules before going on to look at the full protocols on page 97.

When you are working in any public place, or even at home with a room full of people, it is important to block out what you are physically seeing, hearing and touching, as these are all outside

The psychic rules

- In all things, never be attached to the outcome.
- Never look at the sitter or judge them by what they look like or how they are dressed.
- Never question what you first receive in hearing or vision – tell it like it is. The message is for the sitter to understand, not you.
- Do not embellish what you receive with your thinking – one word can speak volumes.
- Once you are in Code A, tell the sitter not to speak unless absolutely necessary. 'Yes' and 'no' are permissible, but nothing more.
- Be calm, warm and friendly with the sitter, and always speak in an upbeat tone.
- Work fast and with a continual flow. Allow no gaps to occur, especially at first.
- Most of all, trust and believe in yourself – you are giving a service.

influences. This includes other people talking and moving around. This will become easier with practice, and practice will in turn engender trust in your ability as you build up your accuracy.

In the exercises you have done so far, you often have to close your eyes. This is in order to prevent you from taking visual hints and making false judgements when you work. Eventually, with practice and growing expertise you can simply move your head slightly to the right (or if you're left-handed, to the left) and allow your eyes to glaze over without actually closing.

USING THE FULL PROTOCOLS

The full protocols are the series of steps that you should always take before and after doing psychic work. You will recognise some of them from Chapter Three. Here I give you the full set.

Using the full protocols, you should now practise tuning in and tuning out with as many people and in as many different circumstances as you can. If possible, use a tape recorder to record your sessions. If you cannot do this, give your sitter a pen and paper and ask them to make a note of your messages – no matter how strange or outlandish these messages may seem. On later reflection, they may turn out to mean a great deal to the sitter. Continue to keep a record until you feel strong enough to give a full 'message service' for at least 20 minutes. For the first four sittings you do, fill in the progress sheet on page 98.

The full protocols

1. If necessary, use the inspirational moment 'psychic takeaway' on page 34 to alter your mood to a positive and happy state.

2. Sit in an upright position in a chair with both feet on the ground, legs uncrossed and relax your shoulders. Make sure all phones, music, computers, TVs and so on are turned off, and that you will not be interrupted.

3. Take three relaxed breaths in and out. Close your eyes and tell your body, 'You are now in a relaxed state and all is well.' If you are still feeling stressed, do the relaxation and self-healing 'psychic takeaway' on page 71.

4. When you are ready, say, 'I am now in Code A.'

5. Say, 'As I raise myself up to the spirit net of love and light, I ask that only the highest may enter. I ask for hearing, vision and feeling to help . . . [sitter's name].' Now start work immediately.

6. Once you have finished working, close down by saying, 'I am now closing down the light. I thank all those who have come in to help me.' Then take a breath and tell yourself, 'I am now back, with no attachment.' Smile and move around.

PROGRESS SHEET

SITTING ONE

Date: .... Name of sitter ....

1. Did you give at least one message?   YES .... NO ....

2. Did the sitter take and understand the
   message?   YES .... NO ....

3. How many messages did you give?   Number: ....

4. Were these messages all accepted and
   understood?   YES .... NO ....

SITTING TWO

Date: .... Name of sitter ....

1. Did you give at least one message?   YES .... NO ....

2. Did the sitter take and understand the
   message?   YES .... NO ....

3. How many messages did you give?   Number: ....

4. Were these messages all accepted and
   understood?   YES .... NO ....

SITTING THREE

Date: .... Name of sitter ....

1. Did you give at least one message?   YES .... NO ....

2. Did the sitter take and understand the
   message?   YES .... NO ....

3. How many messages did you give?   Number: ....

4. Were these messages all accepted and
   understood?   YES .... NO ....

SITTING FOUR

Date: .... Name of sitter ....

1. Did you give at least one message?   YES .... NO ....

2. Did the sitter take and understand the
   message?   YES .... NO ....

3. How many messages did you give?   Number: ....

4. Were these messages all accepted and
   understood?   YES .... NO ....

POSSIBLE PROBLEMS

In column one are some of the problems that may arise until you are fully confident and trusting in your new-found psychic ability. In column two are their solutions.

Problem	Solution
I got nothing at all.	Practise Code A and try again.
My mind chatter wouldn't stop.	Your subconscious will block you if you are not able to stay relaxed and in Code A and will in consequence stop any form of communication. Go back to basics and start again. Practice makes perfect.
I got a message but was too scared to say what I received to the sitter.	Don't be put off. Tell it exactly as it is.
I got more, but didn't say it – it seemed too ridiculous.	Next time tell it all, however silly it sounds to you. Never judge the message.
I heard a message but didn't believe it.	Again, don't judge – just say what you got.
I got a message but it didn't make any sense to me.	Don't let logic get in the way. Ever.
The sitter didn't understand anything I came up with.	Don't be put off. Leave it with them to check names and details later. You may get a surprise!
I got a name but it didn't mean anything.	Ditto the above – but was there anyone else in the vicinity of the sitter at the time to whom it might mean something?
Some things were right, but not others.	Have faith – the others may have yet to happen or to make sense to the sitter.

HOW WILL I KNOW IF IT IS RIGHT TO PASS ON A DIFFICULT MESSAGE?

If you are faced with this question, be sure never to make a personal judgement. Remember, everything in life is difficult and your work is to benefit others and give out messages with honesty and warmth and in as uplifting a way as possible. Allow the wisdom of your guide or of the spirit people to decide what is best for the sitter at that time, for you cannot know that. You are the messenger only, so pass the message on to them with love and kindness, however hard it is for you to do so, and you will become braver.

SHOULD I FEEL SCARED IF I SENSE SOMETHING PHYSICAL?

In principle, the answer to this question is no. If you feel scared, clear yourself by tuning out (see page 97) and giving yourself a 'psychic takeaway' (see page 34). Then re-tune and say (in your mind), 'I am not ready for physical phenomena.' However, if you are getting physical sensations while you are in a place you are not familiar with, it might be appropriate either to leave or to call in, as a command, a protective energy field of light to surround you like a balloon. Say, for example:

> I ask for protection at this time and call in an energy field of white light to surround and safeguard me.

Thereupon you will be safe.

SUE'S STORY: LEARNING TO DEAL WITH OBSESSION

Sue was 23 years old, with a warm, sensitive, fun-loving nature. She exuded great sexual energy and charm, and was never without a lover. Having been brought up in a loving, stable and well-off family who had given her a good education, she found it easy to mix with others and was very popular among her friends. She had trained as an actress and enjoyed a number of successful roles in theatre and TV. Lately, however, she had started suffering from obsessive behaviour and was seeing a sex therapist.

Sue had heard about my work and, having had a session with me, asked if I would train her to be a psychic. She loved the idea and felt it would give her a real purpose in life, as well as helping her to gain control of her sex drive. She was extremely sensitive and felt she needed a technique that would enable her to organise her life better and feel more in control day to day. She also wanted to become a great psychic!

Given the rather chaotic way she was currently running her life, it was obviously going to take a lot of effort on Sue's part to find the time and create the energy to do the training; however, she managed to arrange a date every fortnight when she could come along for a session. I gave her the choice of training either with a small group or alone with me. Being the social mixer she was, Sue decided to work in a group, knowing that I was always prepared to meet with her privately too if there was ever a need.

Sue's training had to be geared to dealing with her personal problems, and involved understanding the trip-switches in her mind, taking true control of her body and re-directing the thoughts that had been giving her an almost continual desire for sex. She worked very hard at the training over several years, and as her life changed, she never looked back. Her greatest feat was building up her self-worth and achieving a sense of completeness. She succeeded in doing this by utilising her sensitivity in positive psychic work and helping others. In the process, she learnt a great about herself and her thoughts and what was causing them to lead her into physical situations she couldn't control.

Sue is now happily married and lives in Scotland. She has become a successful psychic, working with the stars. She continues to work in film and TV too, and also helps people to overcome their own particular obsessions.

I always warn people who have a physical obsession not simply to try to block it. In my opinion, you cannot leave a void, as a void is like a vacuum and will always demand and take more. It is better slowly and steadily to replace the object of the obsession with something more constructive – something that you love and enjoy. In Sue's case it was channelling her energy into becoming a positive spiritual worker. She tells me that to this day she still follows the rules laid out in this book, and whenever necessary uses the affirmations that I gave her for herself – which in turn she now gives to the many people who come to her for help.

 PSYCHIC TAKEAWAY: **GO WITH THE FLOW**

For success in life; for finding whatever you wish for; or for receiving what has been promised and you are expecting to take place . . . or simply would adore if it happened to come to you . . . cut off from your daily thoughts and tell yourself:

Whatever is, I go with the flow. I have no attachment to the outcome.

Now simply let go and relax.

SEEING THINGS AND GETTING A SENSE OF FEELING

6

In this chapter, you will be using your 'inner' and 'outer' psychic vision as much as possible, quite deliberately and purposefully stretching any and every limitation you might presently have. (I explain more about these two kinds of vision below.) The exercises in this chapter are all about denying you the use of your eyes. Whatever you see with your eyes has been shaped by your memory and becomes the means by which you make judgements – so please no cheating by looking when you do the exercises.

During training, most people become more successful in one area than another. If this is already the case for you, that's fine. Many accomplished psychics tend to work with one sense in particular, and you may well find the same. Ideally, however, you are working to create a perfect balance among all the subtle senses. If this has not yet happened, don't worry. With regular practice over the months that balance will be achieved, allowing for 'hearing', 'seeing' and 'feeling' in unison. You'll get there in the end.

TYPES OF CLAIRVOYANCE

As I mentioned above, clairvoyance consists of 'inner' and 'outer' vision. Outer vision refers to when something is seen – subtly – somewhere in front or to the right-hand side of you.

(If you are left-handed, it will be on the left-hand side, due to the reversal of the brain functions.) Inner vision refers to 'seeing' with your eyes closed (at least at first). This kind of vision comes in waves of shapes and colours that form pictures in your head – ever more vividly as you progress. With both types of clairvoyance, your visions may be hazy at first, but over time they will increase in clarity.

An adept can use a further and most exceptional visual tool, the third eye. One of the most incredible aspects of the third eye that I have experienced is its potential to take you on boundless journeys through time and space. Once 'opened' (or activated), 'the eye' can be called upon while you are in Code A. It works rather like a remote sensor or personal video camera, but on the basis of intuitive feeling. I mention this here, as you might have the third eye pop into action any time from now on!

CLAIRVOYANCE, MIND-BENDING AND CHARLATANS

You should be aware that it is incredibly easy to do the human thing and make assumptions based on what you physically see in front of you. Some of TV's mind-magicians have made their names in this way. By carefully studying human behaviour, body language and the use of key words and phrases, they are able to come up with amazing details about the people sitting in their audience. They are entertainers who have indeed learnt their trade well, and it's one of great showmanship I'll admit, but in my opinion they are magicians who practise the craft of illusion only, no more and no less.

I am also aware of people calling themselves psychic who use many such techniques. According to a couple of TV magicians I have talked to, these people sincerely believe all psychic and spiritual work to be pure baloney and so have made it their mission to pillory and debunk all genuine, well-intentioned psychics.

At this point, I am going to digress slightly, because I'd like to tell you about an experience of stage psychism – in this case hypnotism – that I had some years ago.

One day, a friend telephoned me very excitedly to tell me about an incredible one-man show he'd seen on tour that would shortly be coming to a major London theatre. The show boasted the amazing talents of one guy – let's call him Peter Goblin – whose mind had magical powers. He had travelled the world and trained with the greatest masters in Tibet ... and that was just for starters! Apparently, he could bend the minds of any and every unsuspecting volunteer invited onto the stage, making them do ridiculous things totally outside their knowledge or control.

I couldn't resist the temptation, and not only to go along. I wanted to experience first-hand these mind-altering abilities and see whether they were for real or not. I am quite aware that there are many people who are susceptible to suggestion and that they can be led by word patterns, phrases and to some extent sensory bombardment such as touch. If this was the kind of thing Peter Goblin was doing, I wanted to know if he was doing it responsibly and, more to the point, whether he had a technique that could unlock some of the great potential power within the human psyche.

The show duly arrived in town, and with eight other friends I arrived at the theatre door, fully intending to be one of the chosen subjects for that night's show. I used wilful intent and great determination to make sure that I was picked as one of the four to be summoned up on stage, along with another woman and two men.

I spent the first half of the show using all my will to balance the control I needed for myself with the relaxation required to 'play the game' that Peter Goblin was requiring his stage volunteers to play. It wasn't at all easy, I can tell you.

The four of us were summoned up on stage. After some time, Mr Goblin announced to us: 'You are now paralysed and cannot move.' Then he told us, 'I am now going to throw this box of matches to you, and however hard you try, you will not be able to catch it.'

Thankfully, sitting on the end, I was to be the last of the four to be thrown the box, so I had time to prepare. I ordered my body to work under my own instructions and not Mr Goblin's. So while I was telling myself over and over again, 'I can and will catch the box', over and over again, the three others were suffering the most dreadful humiliation as they found themselves completely unable to move their arms, let alone catch the box – much to the growing amazement and amusement of the audience, who were by now definitely in awe of Mr Goblin's power.

Then came my turn and – bingo! – I caught the box. I could see that Peter Goblin was absolutely furious with me. He called immediately for an intermission, whereupon – with the audience unable to see – he marched over to me and punched me in the small of the back. 'What a creep!' I thought, but said not a word.

For the rest of the show I was carefully avoided. I just sat there on the end like a spare part. However, this gave me the chance to observe the three others being played mercilessly for what I could only see as more and more cruel 'entertainment value'. By the end of the show the wonderful Mr Goblin had planted specific commands in the minds of the other woman and the man beside her which both were to react to after the show. Having left the theatre, the man was to start looking desperately for his 'lost gold nugget', asking everyone he came across to assist him, and searching out a policeman to help. The woman was to go home, go to sleep and on waking up the next morning spend the whole day looking manically for her 'lost leprechaun'.

I don't know about you, but I felt a real sense of alarm for the man and woman concerned, and when we all got up to leave the auditorium, I found myself walking behind the duped man. I put my hand on him and asked whether he was aware of his gold nugget. He didn't even look at me. He immediately flipped out and ran off through the crowds, screaming, 'Who's stolen my nugget?' He was moving at such a pace that his poor wife couldn't catch him up. She promptly burst into tears.

I was horrified at what had happened, and by now so was everyone else around us. I was also well aware that the wonderful Mr Goblin had left the proceedings and was long gone.

So we all stood helpless and aghast as this poor man went running off down the middle of the road screaming for help, while the duped girl seemed to be in a wholly mesmerised state – her husband was quite ashen beside her. I've no doubt he was thinking of the morning and dreading what would happen when they both woke up.

Eventually, together with my friends, I arrived back at my flat. I felt strangely alert and full of energy – not excited exactly, but rather as if I was full of a great new awareness. It was really quite spooky. As I sat idly listening to the chatter going on around me, I found myself able to pick up everyone's thoughts to such an extent that I asked them all to shut up and think of a subject, then I told them exactly what they were thinking about. They were all as shocked as I was at my apparently incredible accuracy. However, I just couldn't stop. By now I was viewing everything in their minds to the point that they got rather frightened. To this day, I still remember that feeling in my brain of being a totally open 'receiver'. It was a quite amazing sensation.

Finally, everyone went home, but then, of course, charged up as I was, I didn't want to stop and to sleep. I knew that if and when I did, this incredible openness would close off and I would wake up back to normal again. Which is exactly what happened – thankfully. I would have been a total nightmare to anyone and everyone if what had been activated in my conscious brain that evening had somehow remained switched on.

On reflection, I now believe a good hypnotic subject is one who willingly allows the hypnotist (or therapist) to have control of their subconscious with no sense of fear, reason or logic blocking them doing it. And I, through sheer effort of will, fought any potential take-over of my subconscious – which in turn over-stimulated the power of my consciousness!

PSYCHIC SPEAK LIST

These following are useful words to consider when using your feeling sense to create a visual picture. Ask yourself whether what you are touching is:

Hot / cold
Fast / slow
Moving / still
In colour / black and white / grey
Male / female / both / neither
Happy / sad
Solid / fluid
Indoors / outdoors / distant
Like / dislike
Good feeling / bad feeling / no feeling

WAKE-UP CALL: **BECOMING PHOTO-SENSITIVE**

This exercise involves working with photographs in sealed envelopes (non-transparent ones, of course!). You will be picking up what's on the photo by touching the envelope with your fingers.

Before you start work, you will need to ask a friend to put some photos in sealed envelopes (one photo in each envelope). They should number each envelope and keep a record of which photo corresponds to each number. Make sure they do this well away from your home and that they bring the envelopes to you already sealed. I would suggest you work with only three or four envelopes at any one time.

Again, if possible tape the sessions to keep a record of your training work or get your friend to write down what you come up with – you'll forever be surprised just how much evidence you give out when you listen to them later on. You should also fill in a progress sheet (see page 112) for each photograph.

- Ask your friend to bring one of the envelopes into the room where you will be working. It is vital that you are not confused by information coming from the other envelopes, so make sure they are not in the room and that you only handle one envelope at a time.
- Use the full protocols for preparing to do psychic work (see page 97), but as you do so, direct your mind towards 'seeing' remotely.
- Once you are in Code A, close your eyes, pick up the first envelope and let your fingers sense the vibrations coming through. Report everything you pick up (using the 'psychic speak list' above as a guide), including impressions, feelings and visions. For example: 'The envelope I am picking up feels grey with some green . . . and sad . . .' Do all of this without thinking and without any attachment to the outcome. Work as speedily as you can, letting the impressions flow. When the flow stops, you stop.
- Take a breath, relax. Ask your friend to take away the envelope and bring in the next one.
- When you have finished, use the protocols for closing down.
- Now check your impressions against the photos in each envelope and fill in a progress sheet for each photo.

PROGRESS SHEET

Are you seeing any colours?   YES .... NO ....

If yes, what colours? ....

....

Did you get a vision?   YES .... NO ....

If yes, describe the vision: ....

....

....

....

....

....

What else did you see?
(Even the smallest thing is important.)

I also saw: ....

....

....

....

....

....

....

Did you pick up anything else from the
photo (eg a story behind the picture, a
special place, something that had yet to
happen to whoever or whatever was in
the picture)?   YES .... NO ....

If yes, describe what you picked up: ---

If you have picked up what is in the photo correctly, well done, you
have leapt straight into advanced psychic work. Trust yourself and
keep doing the photo-work to gain as much evidence of your psychic
ability as you can. Congratulations. Keep smiling!

If you had trouble picking anything up, keep trying. Do at least 10
envelopes. If you still have a problem, give yourself a break, then give
yourself an inspirational moment (see the 'psychic takeaway' on page
34) and some relaxation and self-healing (see the 'psychic takeaway'
on page 71), and then have fun trying to do the envelopes again. You
will find you improve each time.

PSYCHOMETRY

Psychometry is the use of the sense of touch to pick up on the residual field left on an object by those who have handled or owned it before. *Objets d'art*, keepsakes, furniture and houses all absorb energy fields that can be sensed, understood and translated by a sensitive. I have found that items made of wood absorb and emit a greater field than any other material, although old pieces of gold and silver jewellery can also hold a great deal of energy, and often have interesting and varied histories.

The walls of old houses and castles also absorb loud or high-pitched sounds. These are what are called 'residual hauntings'; they are buried in the fabric of the building but do not communicate directly – it's more like listening to a recording. For a sensitive it is possible to stand in one of the rooms, go into Code A and literally tune into the 'held' frequency, just like finding a radio station. While on that waveband, not only can you hear the sounds of any traumatic event that took place in the building but you can also see events from that time clairvoyantly. Amazing, eh?

If you decide to check out a spooky place in this way, take a digital tape recorder with you and keep it on. This type of tape recorder will pick up far more sounds than you can, as you will discover when you get back home and play it back! It's fine to go on your own if you have the guts to, but personally I find it more fun to go with several people of the not-scared-witless variety. I also get involved in what I term 'international ghost-busting', mainly due to TV and magazine requests. I make it fun and enjoy every moment, spook or no spook.

WAKE-UP CALL: **PSYCHOMETRY WITH SMALL OBJECTS**

A lot of people have told me they much prefer working with small items to photo-sensing with envelopes – for them it just seems easier. For me, the problem is that you can see the object, which raises the possibility that you will make judgements based on the evidence of your physical vision rather than sensing psychically. So be careful not to jump to conclusions based on what your eyes can see.

Before you do this exercise, you will need to ask friends and family if they can bring you a small item or two to use. Preferably, they should bring old items that have some history, such as a piece of jewellery, a watch, a small antique. However, they must have a good knowledge of the item's past and/or of the previous owner, so that they can verify the information you pick up.

When you first start to do this exercise, you will find the 'psychic speak list' on page 110 helpful. As you develop your psychometric skills, you can allow yourself to start to sense the personality of the owner. Eventually, you will also get an inner vision of the person, whom you can then describe fully.

- Following the protocols on page 97, go into Code A.
- As in the 'wake-up call' for becoming photo-sensitive on page 111, close your eyes, pick up the first object and let your fingers sense the vibrations coming through. Report everything you pick up (using the 'psychic speak list' as a guide), including impressions, feelings and visions.
- When you have finished working with the object, make a record of what you sensed. Once you have had a chance to verify your findings with its owner, you should also note down whether your impressions were accurate.
- When you have finished with all your objects, follow the protocols for closing down

Do this exercise 20 or so times. By that time, you should have gained confidence in your ability and should be having nothing but hits. However, if you find you are having lots of misses, go back to basics and try again.

THE COLOUR CODE

While you are working with psychic sensing, you may find it useful to check out the following colour chart, which you can refer to in conjunction with the stripes of colour printed on the inside of this book's cover. Each colour has a different vibration. A speedy vibration gives off a sense of heat and is stimulating, whereas a slow vibration feels cold and tends to slow you down.

All colours – be they in your home, around you on the street or in your clothes – naturally resonate with your physical being, even if you only see them subliminally. To a greater or lesser extent, all of these colours will have an effect on your everyday life.

Colours and their vibrations

Red

- The speediest vibration
- Works on the subconscious mind to stimulate a physical drive, eg eating, drinking, exercise, sex
- Represents the material world, eg money
- Great for: physical competitions, games, dancing the night away, keeping warm, feeling sexual, attracting a sexual partner
- Bad for: anger and tantrums, binge-drinking, bouts of violence (in all of which, you already 'see red')

Orange

- Stimulates the desire to spend money – to buy the book, food, make-up, stereo or whatever your subliminal vision has its eye on
- Great for: a day out, walking, going for lunch (you're paying), a shopping spree, selling any goods
- Bad for: saving money, sleep, rest, keeping calm

Yellow

- Stimulates brain activity, triggering the intellect, active thought and conversation
- Great for: business meetings, lively chatty house parties, stimulating talk
- Bad for: those under pressure, those suffering too much emotion, stress, migraines

Green

- Stimulates a feeling of springtime
- Pleases the mind, promotes re-growth and friendship
- Associated with prime of life, excellent for regeneration of body cells and tissue
- Great for: meeting people, presenting speeches, attracting friend-ships, group therapy sessions, healing burns
- Bad for: fast activity, sales packaging, any cancers

Blue

- Creates feelings of peace and tranquillity
- Slows the mind and body, aiding sleep and allowing the body's own healing mechanisms to be activated
- Represents unconditional love and femininity
- Great for: re-energising if tired, creating tranquillity in the home, benefiting the healing process in hospitals, keeping your temper and staying cool, visualisation work
- Bad for: clubbing, physical competitions, fast activity of mind or body

Note: The colours are all in their brightest, strongest form, untainted by any darker shading, which would cause a negative influence.

Colours with no vibration

Black

- The void, the darkness of night
- Strictness, formality
- When worn alone, blocks any attraction from others; if there is lots of flesh showing, has the opposite effect, attracting people to the bare flesh
- Great for: not being noticed in a crowd, hibernation, a Goth party
- Bad for: depression, illness, making announcements, celebrations

White

- No colour
- Represents the power and energy of light
- Gives a visual impression of purity, cleanliness and, when worn alone, virginity (hence for Christian weddings)
- Often worn by those with self-esteem or even self-importance
- Great for: showing off other colours, as a background for designs for clean living, a sense of peace, spiritual upliftment, hot weather
- Bad for: hiding in a crowd, cold weather, being lost in snow!

Grey

- No vibration
- Represents a sense of self-denial, gives out message 'I am not worthy'
- Associated with uniforms, female attire in Christian religious orders, mourning
- Great for: staying unnoticed, looking strict and puritanical; if you're a rabbit!
- Bad for: activity, depression, presentations, dating

Colour mixes

Turquoise

- Wonderfully bright; says 'I shine – see me, hear me'
- Worn by those with courage and self-esteem
- Great for: speeches, parties, important functions, stimulating mind and body, being seen and heard, holiday clothes
- Bad for: stimulating appetite for food

Peach

- Resonates warmth and joy
- Uplifting for the mind and body
- Creates a feeling of calm and happiness
- Great for: clothes that lift the spirits, a 'happy' space in the home
- Bad for: sombre occasions, being taken seriously, being noticed

Brown

- Resonates with the Earth – and earth complements all bright colours and the qualities that go with them
- Mentally and physically grounding
- Conveys a comforting sense of monastic silence and mental discipline
- Great for: serious talk, as a complement to other colours in decorative schemes, feeling secure, homeliness, looking conservative; if you're a chocolate!
- Bad for: speeches, sales packaging

Violet

- Resonates with the Earth's boundary with other dimensions
- The rainbow's end
- Deep violet represents spiritual enlightenment and as such is not widely used in everyday life, in the home, in the office or in fashion, but is used by the Church for specific ceremonies
- Great for: ceremonial garb, being taken very seriously, packaging, anything spiritual or psychic, meditation
- Bad for: new friendships, business meetings, depression

Pink

- Lightens the mind, lifts mood and aids balance
- Very calming
- Great for: children (use in bedrooms of over-active kids) and adults with mental disabilities, peace of mind, prison cells, clean living, a sense of peace, spiritual upliftment, cooling in hot weather
- Bad for: extreme sports, advertising, mentally active work

Sensing colour by touch

You will be amazed at how easy it is to recognise colours by touch alone through their different rates of vibration. For example:

- Red has the speediest vibration. It is stimulating and warming and will sometimes be sensed as physically hot.
- Bright orange is also physically warming. It stimulates and can sometimes feel mentally disturbing.
- Bright yellow activates the intellect, creating a sense of wakefulness. It exudes a warmth and can create a feeling of going out into bright sunlight.
- Emerald green slows you down. It gives a sense of coolness and peace.

WAKE-UP CALL: **THE FIVE KEY COLOUR CARDS 1**

For this exercise you will be making up your own colour cards. You will then be using the cards to sense colour through touch. If possible, record your results or ask a friend to write them down.

You will need: Five sheets of paper (A5 will be big enough), one in each of the five key colours (red, blue, yellow, orange and green); a small bag; a blindfold.

- Cut two postcard-sized shapes out of each piece of paper, then put them in the bag, mix them up well and put them on a table in front of you. (Do not look in the bag.)

- Put on a blindfold, use the protocols (see page 97) to go into Code A.

- Take one card out of the bag at random and touch it with your fingers to get a good sense of the vibration emitted. Continue doing this until you start to sense the vibration, but stop after two minutes, even if you have sensed nothing. Try using the following 'sensitive speak' to translate your impressions into colours:

  - Fast: red, orange
  - Slow: blue, green
  - Hot: red, orange
  - Cool: blue
  - Uneasy: orange

  - Peaceful: green
  - Mentally and/or physically stimulating: yellow, red, orange
  - Regenerating: green
  - Still: blue

You may also 'see' a flash of colour through your inner vision, or you may see a scene characterised by a distinctive colour. For example, you might see a bright red flash or green grass; feel cold or get an impression of sunshine.

- Repeat the exercise with each of the cards. When you have finished, use the protocols to close down (see page 97).

- Now check your accuracy.

WAKE-UP CALL: **THE FIVE KEY COLOUR CARDS 2**

- Follow all the steps for method one, but this time, when you pick a card from the bag, take a breath, relax and put the card against your fore-head, above the bridge of your nose. Leave it there for one minute, noticing any colour vibrations that come to your attention, then put it down. Don't allow yourself more than a minute, even if you haven't yet sensed any vibration.

- Repeat this procedure with each of the cards, picking them out of the bag at random, then close down and check your accuracy as in method one.

  I have found that about 25 per cent of the people I've taught pick up more easily through method two. This method utilises the third eye, which is located where you place the cards, on the forehead. If you got nothing from either method, your senses are blocked. Go back to basics and then repeat the exercise.

  If you find this exercise difficult, don't lose heart. Very few of us can be successful in all areas. While some psychics are great at sensing colours, objects and photographs through psychometry and go on to specialise in clairsentience, others find that their gifts lie in other areas of psychism.

  You can also try repeating the 'wake-up call' for becoming photo-sensitive on page 111 using the colour strips.

KATE'S STORY

Kate was someone who, during her training, found it especially difficult to sense colours psychically. She was 22 and demon-strated a grounded practical approach to life. She had a warm generous nature, and I was impressed by her ability to speak up for herself.

Having come from a very large family with little money to spare, Kate was used to a lot of hard physical work. She had just completed training as a riding instructor and wanted to work with people and animals – especially, of course, horses. I first got to know her when she accepted a job at my stables (where she eventually became the head) and came to live in at my home.

You could say that Kate came to psychic work by accident, except I don't accept that anything in life is ever accidental, rather a product of synchronicity. She had always been fascinated by anything psychic and was intrigued by paranormal 'mysteries'. I also believe that when you work, live or spend time with a psychic person, their psychism tends to rub off on you. This was certainly the case with Kate. Over the number of years that she worked for me, she quietly observed my work with clients (human and animal). Eventually, she asked to train with me. She was particularly keen to become a healer, having a desire to help people and animals.

Kate put her whole heart into her training, but however hard she tried, she found 'seeing' photographs in envelopes and picking up on colour vibrations very difficult. As a result, she started to feel that she wasn't good enough and lost confidence. However, this was soon to change, when she triggered an amazing talent way beyond 'feeling'.

I was in London for the week and Kate was overseeing everything at the farm, including the horses, dogs, cats, geese and chickens. On Monday night she had just gone to bed, when suddenly she became aware of a man standing in the corner of the room looking directly at her. He was dressed in army uniform, and she knew he was an officer, although she was not sure of what rank. Gradually, as Kate watched, a complete image formed around him. He was standing on a lawn with a large mulberry tree nearby. A woman in army uniform was walking towards him. Then, pointing at his left leg, he told Kate, 'You must tell Angela to telephone; it's very urgent.' And then 'Tell Angela,' he said again.

Kate knew without a shadow of doubt that I was the Angela in question and that she had to contact me, so she quickly wrote down all the details so that she could pass them on.

When I got her phone call the next morning, I too wrote down every detail. On questioning, Kate said she thought the man could have been a younger version of my father (whom she had met once), but she couldn't and didn't understand the significance of what she had seen or the message she had given me. In fact, she was very apologetic about it all, but had felt compelled to pass the message on as soon as she could.

What Kate didn't know was that my father had been an officer in the army. The woman in her vision I could easily recognise as my godmother, a friend of my father's who had also been in the army and who had passed over years earlier.

At the time, my father was alive and being cared for in a hospital in Scotland, where he had been laid up for a couple of months, so I immediately telephoned there, feeling sure he must have some sort of serious health problem. A nurse told me that my father was about to have some tests but that he would pass on my love as soon as he saw him.

I took a deep breath and told the nurse what had happened (only I said it was me that had had the vision, as I didn't want to implicate Kate unnecessarily) and demanded that he put a large note on my father's test-sheets asking the doctors to check for any potential problem in his left leg – perhaps thrombosis. I was surprised and delighted that the nurse didn't think I was mad. In fact, he said he believed in psychic messages and promptly promised to do as I requested.

By the end of the day, I still hadn't heard anything, so I phoned the hospital again. A different nurse told me to call back in the morning as there was no further news. Wednesday morning came and I phoned back, and yet another nurse answered. She said she couldn't find my father's notes. I replied that I would hold on until she did. After much rustling, eventually she found the notes and told me that all the tests were clear. However, she couldn't find the note of my request for an examination of his left leg, and I was told to call back later if I wanted to know more. When I did so, I was again told that nothing was wrong with him. Nevertheless, I continued to put pressure on the hospital staff to check his leg. By now I was feeling restless and perturbed about the whole affair, but I knew I could do no more than keep sending my father my love.

Thursday morning arrived and I phoned again. This time, however, the nurse checked my name and asked who I was. An official-sounding voice then came on the line and said, 'Haven't you received a call from us ...? I'm terribly sorry but your father died earlier this morning. It was a suspected heart attack . . .'

The feeling of deep loss hit me like a stone. It was as if I'd been cheated. A sense of complete uselessness flooded all over me. Very soon, however, I managed to pull myself together and recall some comforting memories. In recent years, my father had confided in me that he had been visited by old friends he knew to be dead. He had also seen his dearly beloved dog, Susie, walking around in full health after her actual death. Given his connection with animals, it seemed on reflection Kate had been the perfect messenger between the two of us.

That my father had communicated in the way he did, indicated to me that he was already partly out of body at the time – or, in other words, that he was slipping in and out of life.

Whether it was to some extent a result of the drugs he was on I can't be sure, but certainly his mind had been slowly going and he had been sleeping more and more – to me sure signs of a soul that is no longer fully in this life.

I was grateful to have had the chance to give him my love and blessing – which, I know, helped him feel safe when passing over. I believe his leg, the possible thrombosis and suspected heart attack were his way of 'going', and he actually gave Kate that message. It wasn't for me to alter what was meant to be; my father simply wanted me to know in advance of time. He did so through Kate because it was much too difficult for him to contact me directly with such a message – there was too great an emotional tie between us.

It is worth mentioning here that when such a strong bond is involved – with a close friend or family member – it is very difficult, if not impossible, to release that attachment and become objective. This attachment will tend to block your ability to involve yourself psychically, as you will constantly be trip-switching subconscious emotions.

As for Kate, she did eventually become a good psychic. She much enjoys mediumship, sits in circles for psychic development and gets involved in ghost-busting whenever she can. However, her greatest passion has continued to be healing. She eventually trained with the National Federation of Spiritual Healers (NFSH) and now spends a lot of time giving healing to horses, dogs and people alike. She has also become a great psychic networker, helping people and their animals with their problems across the UK. And she still manages to run a busy home, care for her two children, look after her dogs and give riding instruction as well.

(For more information about the NFSH, see the Resources section on page 235.)

HIDE AND SEEK

What do people do when they realise they have lost something – for example their keys or their wallet? They fly into a panic and rush round making desperate attempts to find it. But that's not what you are going to do from now on. Once you have perfected the psychic search technique, not only will you be able to find your car keys, but you will also be able to retrieve items that have been missing for years . . . or even find your friend's lost cat. Eventually, you will actually be able to locate a missing person – although at this stage, it will be an advanced enough exercise if you simply arrange with family and friends to get someone to hide and then have you pinpoint exactly where they are in the vicinity.

Before you do any of this hide-and-seek work, however, here is some information on how to restore your energy levels.

REPLENISHING YOUR ENERGY

The fact is that all of us suffer tiredness at some time or other, what with late nights, early mornings, mental stress and physical exhaustion due to our hectic and demanding lifestyles. Eventually, if you don't get enough sleep to recharge the battery, your immune system starts to fail, which is when all sorts of nasty bugs can get a hold.

But what no one's probably told you before is that you can attract boundless energy whenever you need it.

WAKE-UP CALL: **ENERGY SOURCING**

In this exercise, you will be using an imaginary pyramid to replenish your energy. Let me explain how it works. While the Earth is constantly giving out positive energy to the universe, the pyramid is like a magnetic device that continually draws energy back in – as do many of the ancient sites such as Stonehenge and Machu Picchu. You could equally well imagine one of these sites for this exercise, but I find that the pyramid works best for me.

The light bobbles in this exercise are there for protection, so please don't forget about them – they are necessary. As I have already explained, there are negative as well as positive energy forces all around you, unseen by the naked eye. Although they cannot be seen, they can be sensed – an example would be the inexplicable feeling of coldness that suddenly goes right through you, as in the old saying, 'Someone just walked over my grave'. So protect yourself and make sure that nothing can invade your space.

You can do this 'wake-up call' indoors or in the garden, or you can do it in a park, as long as there are no distractions.

You will need: A compass (if you don't know the lie of the land).

- Stand facing south (use the compass to find it if you don't know) and go into Code A.
- Imagine that there is a violent thunderstorm going on in the background. The thunderstorm continues throughout the exercise.
- Now mentally create a cinema screen in front of you with a bright blue surround.
- Create a huge pyramid on the screen, with one of its four sides facing you.

- Now, in your mind, give yourself the following commands. Tell yourself that you are stepping out of your body in front of yourself and facing the screen. Around you are bobbles of white protective light.
- Imagine a golden tube attached to the centre of the pyramid. Open your solar plexus (just below your chest) and see the other end of the tube attached to your body there. It is sucking energy from the pyramid and pouring it into you – rather like a petrol pump filling up a car. Keep the energy coming rapidly.
- When you feel full, stop and step back into your body.
- Stop the thunderstorm, wipe the cinema screen and come out of Code A. Take a breath and open your eyes. You have now completely replenished yourself with wonderful, useable energy.

This increased energy is another form of self-empowerment. It will significantly benefit you to generate it before doing any psychic work – not least when friends and family have spread the word and you find yourself suddenly inundated with requests for readings, searches and other help. It takes energy to tune in, do the work and tune out – and to feel empowered enough to say no when you really don't feel up to it or it's not the right situation!

FINDING THINGS THE PSYCHIC WAY

When you lose something and you're in a rush it's always difficult to avoid going into panic mode. However, if you can learn to stop, take a breath and give it thought, you will find that the two psychic methods described below – the screen method and the compass method – are much quicker and far less stressful than running around like a headless chicken emptying drawers and cupboards willy-nilly.

WAKE-UP CALL: **FINDING AN OBJECT – THE SCREEN METHOD**

With your new-found energy, now is the perfect time to have a go at seeking out hidden objects. Before you start the exercise, you should ask someone you trust to hide something you own and have agreed upon – for example keys, a piece of jewellery or a small item from somewhere in your home. Ask them to put it somewhere in a designated room while you wait outside. Once they have done, they should remain totally silent and still until the exercise is over. When you have tried both this method and the following 'compass' method, you should fill in the progress sheet on page 132.

- Enter the room and sit down on a chair. Close your eyes and use the protocols to go into Code A (see page 97).

- Once again, create in your mind the cinema screen with the bright blue surround.

- Project the hidden object onto the screen . . . Now see what you sense around the object. Ask yourself:
  - Is the object somewhere light or dark?
  - Is it somewhere high or low?
  - Is it somewhere colourful or surrounded by nothingness.
  - What textures surround it – wood, metal, material, plastic, leather, glass?
  - What else do you see? (You may get a flash vision or receive a prompt telling you where the object is.)

- The moment you get your answer, *say it*. Trust what you have received. Then stop and go through the protocols for closing down.

- Now check your result with the hider.

WAKE-UP CALL: **FINDING AN OBJECT – THE COMPASS METHOD**

- Once again, ask a trusted person to conceal an object in a designated room.

- Enter the room, close your eyes and use the protocols to go into Code A (see page 97).

- Now you are going to use your body as a compass. Carefully turn around three times on the spot – clockwise if you are right-handed, anti-clockwise if you are left-handed.

- Now allow your body to sense where the object is, letting your right (or left if you are left-handed) arm move like a compass needle until it settles on a point that feels right. Go for it, trust the moment and say where the object is. Then stop and use the protocols for closing down.

- Check your result with the hider and fill in the progress sheet on page 132.

You can use either of these two methods to help people find their lost wallets, keys and jewellery. When you're ready, you can move on to stolen mobiles, handbags, cars, etc. (You will not have to decide when you're ready, by the way. That time has been set and is the moment you're asked, so just trust and go for it.) Don't then put yourself under any pressure. Always tell the person you are doing the search for that you will help them to the best of your ability, but make no promises.

PROGRESS SHEET

1. Did you get the location of the object
    right?   YES .... NO ....

2. Did both methods work equally well?   YES .... NO ....

3. If no, which method worked better and
    why?

If you found the object successfully, congratulations. You are
commanding your will successfully, going with the flow and
remaining unattached to the outcome. You are doing extremely well.

If you found the object with one method but not the other, great –
well done. You may find this will be your preferred method of working, but for the time being keep trying both ways, as it could be that
you are blocking one with your thinking (for example, 'I can't see it'
or 'I don't trust myself').

If you didn't find the object by either method, you probably know what I'm going to say now . . . Give yourself an inspirational moment (see the 'psychic takeaway' on page 34) and give yourself some relaxation and self-healing (see the 'psychic takeaway' on page 71) and then go for it again. Different days create different moods, so you might find it helpful to wait a day or two, but keep trying. Don't let your subconscious block your growing power.

I well understand from my own experience that training yourself to be the best in the many facets of psychic work requires tremendous ongoing effort, especially controlling your mind (perhaps for the first time) and learning truly to believe in yourself and your new abilities. It is a highly intimate and personal process, and it takes time – time allowing 'sensing' to be part of your daily life both at home and at work – to make positive progress.

LOST ANIMALS

If someone say phones you up desperate to find their lost cat or dog, the screen method can be very useful, as it can cover any distance. You should ask for the basic, specific details only, no more and no less:

- The address where the animal went missing.
- The date and time the animal went missing.
- The breed, colour, sex and name of the pet.

Write down everything you are told (without elaborating it in any way). Time is of the essence in tracking down animals (due to human and physical factors). If the animal has been missing for more than two weeks, the trail may have gone cold, and you should warn the owner that this may be the case.

Once you have all the information you need, ask the person to call back in about an hour's time and get to work.

WAKE-UP CALL: **FINDING A LOST ANIMAL BY THE SCREEN METHOD**

You will need: A pen and paper.

● Use the protocols (see page 97) to prepare and go into Code A.

● Using the information you have gathered from the owner, create a screen (as described in screen method 'wake-up call' on page 130) and project the missing animal onto it.

● Using your third eye, endeavour to see the animal leaving the property. Follow the animal in your mind. The journey may be patchy, but you should be able to pick up significant 'clips', as you would on fast film footage, for example landmarks, signs, the countryside, roads, houses. You may also get a prompt. This might be a distance, say of say 200 metres away, or it might be the name of an area, town or city. Write down everything you get – every detail – without allowing your thinking to cut in.

● Pass on everything you have 'seen' to the animal's owner. Be sure to give them absolutely everything, as even small details may be significant.

WAKE-UP CALL: **FINDING A LOST ANIMAL BY THE COMPASS METHOD**

This method can be used if you have an idea of the area where the missing animal can be found and are yourself able to go out and search. Personally, I have found it easier to use this method at night, when there are fewer distractions to block out the information I am receiving. The most important thing is to trust your ability and connect to the lost animal with love. Do the work with joy for the giving, and I wish you every success from my heart and soul.

- Go to the place where the animal was last seen or where you have a sense it may have been.

- Use the protocols (see page 97) to go into Code A.

- Following the directions in the compass method 'wake-up call' on page 131, use your right arm (left arm if you are left-handed) as a compass to indicate the direction in which the animal went. Keep following your compass until you sense that you've reached the correct spot. Believe me, it will be so strong that you will know how far to go. Of course, you will need to open your eyes so as not to fall over roots and stones or blunder into lamp-posts and trees, but try to keep your physical eyes unfocused and hazy and your head slightly tilted to the side as you work. This will help you to remain open and unblocked. Do not allow any verbal or mental chatter while you are working.

- When you have finished your search, use the protocols to close down (see page 97) and return the animal to its owner.

JANE GOLDMAN'S TELEVISION EVIDENCE

A few years ago, I worked as mentor/adviser on a TV series presented by Jane Goldman, which was sold to numerous countries worldwide, including the USA. The idea behind the TV series was for Jane to investigate the main areas of psychic work and to observe and test the many techniques used by psychics in the UK.

Jane was first and foremost a researcher and journalist, with neither a ready belief in nor acceptance of the psychic world. It was my job to teach her to work psychically herself. I gave her the basic training covered in this book, up to and including the exercises in this chapter. And I have to say she surprised herself, let alone the production team, with her accuracy when put to the test finding lost objects. She succeeded in working with both methods accordingly, and watching her as she realised she could do it was great TV.

She also successfully managed to match a watch to its owner by picking out the correct sealed envelope. Admittedly, I was there reminding her to trust what she was sensing, but I never once gave her any other tips or assistance as she carried out the exercise on camera.

Later on in the series, I took Jane to a house where I had lived as a child. Although she did not train long enough to learn how to 'see' ghost people, nevertheless, she accurately pinpointed a specific room where a ghost was *in situ* – not bad considering that there were over 20 rooms to choose from! This was also the episode that got the show's parapsychologist excited, as the thermometer he was using went into overdrive.

SPIRIT GUIDES

Each 'wake-up call' you complete successfully will wake up a few more of your psychic abilities, enhancing your whole being. As this happens your spirit teachers and guides will start to move in and draw other experiences towards you. Take it from me, they will know well before you do what you are ready for next – and that is what will take place, whatever you think about it. Learning to be a psychic is an absorbing journey of continuous learning. With every event you encounter, you will acquire a greater understanding.

Down over the years, I have had many lessons from my own spirit teachers, all of whom have patiently explained much to me, and always with a deep love and wisdom that may not have been fully apparent to me at the start. Because they don't work by spoon-feeding. They won't just give you the answers, but will make sure that you work them out yourself, so that you increase your awareness and learn the lesson properly first time around.

Take a moment to visualise another dimension, akin to the physical one you already know so well, yet operating at a higher resonance than the one you are in. While its very essence is beyond the capacity of human physical vision and hearing, nevertheless it encompasses the whole universe, including planet Earth. And it has many levels. Spirit people who have chosen to work with the living do so from the closest level to Earth, but they do so without attachment. They are not stuck here and can come and go, returning to their higher 'home' level as and when they desire.

Compatibility is everything in working with a spirit guide – human being and spirit must be on the same wavelength. While your guide (or guides) could come from any era or place, usually they will come from roughly the same time frame as you – roughly within a century. This is because to be most useful for you they have to be able to empathise with you and communicate in a way you can understand. Usually, this communication will come through telepathic prompts. It will also be pitched at a level that is right for you, so if your chosen journey in this life is one of seeking spiritual awareness and progression, you are likely to have a guide who is a very learned being. So the appropriate guide for you may be more spiritually advanced than another one working with an individual who hasn't yet reached the same stage as you.

I have found help from such guides at times when I wished to know more about a specific subject, for example where we originated from beyond planet Earth. In answer to this question, my guide slowly shook his head in a knowing manner, while impressing upon me that I would know in time, but now I must wait. So patience and trust continue to be foremost in my mind!

The expression 'horses for courses' comes to mind where guides are concerned. Some years ago, I arrived home, turned on the radio and caught the end of an interview. A composer, Howard Blake, was talking about how one day he was walking with his children across a field in Cornwall, in the south-west of England, when he received, through 'hearing', an amazing piece of music. He ran back to their cottage and wrote it all down. It was the music for the well-known children's animated film *The Snowman*. I was so delighted to hear this that I put out the wish to meet this man. A year later, a student unexpectedly told me, 'You have to meet a close friend of mine, Howard Blake; he connects to all you do.' Needless to say, we met soon after that. But my point is, Howard Blake knew without a shadow of doubt that he received all his best work via the spirit net and that he had had a brilliant composer as one of his guides.

So whether your guide is a Chinese sage, an Indian guru, a doctor or a businessman, they will be there to suit the specific journey you have chosen in this life.

Once you have progressed further in your psychic work, your guide will be able to work with you in many more progressive ways. He may allow you to see him or to hear him whenever the need arises. The speech of spirit guides is known as 'outer voice'. It utilises the void between sound waves called 'mush' or 'white noise', which is rather like the sound of running water or the gaps between radio stations.

Every living being has one or more guides, although most are unaware of them and would never think of summoning them during their normal everyday lives. But these guides are always on call, so to speak, ready for a particular moment of need or for a time of life when an openness towards the spiritual has been reached. I hear many stories of people who had no spiritual beliefs until they encountered a close call with death. At that moment they prayed instinctively to a higher being or force of some kind – and, bingo, they survived! Others have gone through a near-death experience, being taken up to the spirit levels, with their guide, to see and sense the afterlife for themselves. This is often a wonderful experience, in which they are able to meet up with loved ones who have passed away. However, if some shock tactic is required, it can be just the reverse. In this case, the person is shown what can be expected at the much lower levels.

A LIFE OF SERVICE AND SPIRITUAL GROWTH

As you develop and use your power, remember you are giving a service to others – although in exchange for that service you will find your life is enormously enriched. Alterations and shifts will take place, sometimes quite dramatic ones. After all, you are changing yourself by way of increasing your psychic field, and the positive energy field that results will be understood and felt by those around you, even if in subtle ways.

As this energy field increases through your ongoing work, you will find you are attracting new people towards you. Many will be like-minded sensitives, but others will seek your assistance only. Some – perhaps even old friends – may not be able to stay with you on your journey, as it makes them feel uncomfortable or unsafe. These will be people who cannot easily or willingly move out of the confines of their own belief system. Don't judge them for that. If what you are doing is not to their liking or 'choosing', it is far better to let them go and allow them to follow their own journey.

Being the best is really about your innermost soul making the most spiritually out of the period of time allotted to you on Earth. This means using each and every opportunity in the moment it arrives as well as (possibly the greatest challenge of all) walking your talk on your spiritual path, even if it takes you where others fear to tread.

But take heart. The following are spiritual sayings I some-times use:

- A true giver is a happy receiver.
- If you love the idea, it is not hard to do.

- True love comes from within and emits the greatest warmth.
- Live in the moment, for the moment.
- The subconscious chatter that restricts your true horizons and goals also dictates your ultimate happiness.
- A drop of kindness shared gives you a glow like no other.

SO HOW ARE YOU DOING?

A timely question perhaps? If you are getting results and progressing well, congratulations. That's wonderful. However, don't worry if you are having difficulty in achieving the results you expect or if, going on the results you've got to date, you are not sure you're doing all the work correctly. It takes great energy to develop the knowledge you need and a leap of faith to trust that knowledge. There will be many plateaus, slips and mistakes along the way. Some may feel that they're not progressing fast enough, others may be annoyed or frustrated that they can't get it right all the time, while still others may question whether they've even succeeded at all – but these are all natural reactions and to be expected. You can't reach Olympic standards overnight!

If you have fallen into any of these states of mind, I recommend that you put the book down and leave it alone for a week or two to clear your mind and shift your mood, then come back to it afresh. Your brain will have been working away quietly in the interim, sorting things out and opening up the necessary new connections. What seemed an insurmountable problem before, should by then have become nothing more than a hiccup along the way.

DEALING WITH ATTACHMENT TO GOALS

One of the problems that sometimes crops up in psychic training is becoming attached to the goals that you set yourself. These may be goals in the actual work (for example to achieve 100 per cent results with a particular exercise) or they may be goals in your wider life (for example to get a new job, buy a new home or find a new relationship). There are several ways in which you can deal with this:

- Ask yourself why you want to achieve the goal you've set yourself. Work out what you *really* want. What does the goal represent for you?

- Leave things open for your highest good rather than limiting yourself to a specific goal – be it a job, a home or relationship you are looking for. (And be aware that you should never ask for anything that is to the detriment of any other living being.)

- Be aware of the good things you have now. Use phrases such as: 'I have the perfect work' and 'I have an abundance of wealth', then add 'in the most divine way'.

- Build up positive energy with happy thoughts and a smile. This will strengthen your self-worth so that you really trust what you're doing. Then take a breath and release your goal fully from your mind – really let it go, which means not giving thought to it again. And then shift yourself. Do something else straightaway to expunge the old goal from your mind.

PSYCHIC TAKEAWAY: **STAYING GROUNDED AND DOING THE WORK**

How do you remain grounded in day-to-day realities and do this work? You do it with a concerted effort of will – in other words, by command.

Remind yourself that you are the one in charge, and make it part of your daily life to do so.

Only tune in and out when necessary.

As a result of doing the exercises in this book, your lifestyle will alter for the better, allowing scope for your new-found work as a psychic.

So wherever you go and whatever you do in your day, if you feel yourself in a light-headed daze or in the wrong place at the wrong time, take a few deep breaths, clench your fists a couple of times and physically shift yourself. This is grounding and will allow you time to gain control.

AERIAL VIEW 8

How do you become a great seer, journeying to paranormal realms far across time and space?

Some say the future can be determined by studying history – that the same scenarios of war, peace and other such events recur in a cyclical manner and therefore become predictable. But this kind of prediction is limited to the capabilities of the rational brain, and you will be working way beyond them, with a belief and understanding that anything and everything is possible.

The work you have done up to now will have shown you the boundless potential of the journey you're on, so in many senses you have gone most of the distance already. Before you sit back and rest on your laurels, however, you should at least find out just how much further you can go by letting your third eye take over the next stage of your journey.

THE THIRD EYE

To me, the third eye is the most dazzling and exciting extra-sensory faculty of the human vessel. In a way, unleashing it is like letting the genie out of the bottle, with the difference that the third eye is kept under strict control through your own thought-commands. As I have already mentioned (see page 59), the third eye – or 'eye' – lies dormant (in most of us) above the bridge of the nose between the eyes. In your case, however, the 'wake-up calls' you have already completed will have awakened and activated it. Now I'm going to tell you how to put it to work by command.

WAKE-UP CALL: **THE AERIAL VIEW**

In this exercise, you will going on a journey; however, it is your 'eye' that will be doing the travelling, taking you to places beyond most people's wildest imaginings in no time at all. In real time, the journey will take a few seconds, as your 'eye' needs to acclimatise itself on arrival at the destination.

As I have repeated many times, you must never have any attachment to a particular outcome. When doing this exercise, do not connect your-self in any way to what you see. The best words to use in this respect are: 'I am viewing', 'I see', 'I sense'.

The past, present and future are all defined and separated in time, but because in this exercise you will be journeying beyond time, the only way to know exactly what period you are in is to look around for tell-tale signs, for example a calendar, a newspaper, billboard or some other clue – a horse-drawn carriage or a motorcar, period or modern dress, etc.

Before you do this exercise, you will need to ask a friend to pick a specific well-known site somewhere in the world, for example the Eiffel Tower, the Tower of London, Sydney Opera House. Whatever site they pick, they must either know it or have a picture of it for accuracy. Ask them to write the name and address, including the country, on a piece of paper, fold it and seal it in an envelope. They should preferably do this somewhere away from you and then bring it to you when you do the exercise.

You will need: A large piece of unlined paper and a pen.

- Close your eyes and use the protocols to go into Code A (see page 97).
- Put a hand on the envelope and direct your thoughts to it. Ask in your mind to see the site named in the envelope. If you feel blocked, take a breath and move your head slightly.
- Whatever comes into focus, write it down.

- Move around the room if you need to – you don't have to be stuck in one place. Then ask to see more.
- If you get a complete vision, try drawing the significant shapes, landmarks and so on. (You don't have to be a great artist.)
- When you have seen all there is to see, you have finished.
- Use the protocols to tune out (see page 97) and take a breath.
- Now fill in the progress sheet below.

 PROGRESS SHEET

Did you only draw the correct shape of the landmark?	5 points	YES	NO ....
Did you recognise the place you saw and write it down?	10 points	YES	NO ....
Did you draw the whole site correctly?	10 points	YES	NO ....

5 points	Well done.
10 points	Congratulations.
Nothing	Try again at a different time, with a different site. Keep trying. It's always worth it.

MY EXPERIENCES WITH THE AERIAL VIEW

On one occasion, I was asked to view a certain city in China on a particular date in 2025. Wow, I thought! What fun! And off I went, flying high above the city, rather as if I was in a helicopter but a much smoother ride. Most big cities look a bit alike from above, so I had to search for specific landmarks and zoom in to see actual people. Then my sensing came into play.

Many times in this book I have told you never to judge what you see or hear but just to go with the flow and trust . . . Yet when I'd finished this particular journey I was more than a bit upset.

There was great clarity in my glimpse of this moment in the future. It was a warm sunny day, there were no clouds or wind, the city had no smog and all the buildings seemed clean and in good order. But it was eerily quiet everywhere I looked or went. There were no traffic jams: indeed, there were no trucks, buses or even cars on the roads as you would expect. In fact, the only vehicle I saw was an old, worn-out, red pick-up parked up on the side of an otherwise empty main street.

And worse, there were so few people – less than a handful slowly moving about the city, one of them an old man tottering around on a bicycle. Something was badly wrong. The more I looked, the more it seemed that the place was recovering from some terrible silent upheaval that had left everything neat and tidy and undamaged, but empty and lifeless at the same time. It was not a nice view.

There was more, of course, but I'm not going to go into that here. What you should know is that when you journey with the third eye, you have an acute awareness of everything you see, a 'knowing' if you like. And while all that you have seen will seem to disappear on your return, if you later give thought to the experience, everything will come flooding back and you can re-live the whole encounter in full detail.

This journey, together with numerous other visions of future events that I have had, begs the question whether everything is written in advance of time. Can you change it if you have already seen the outcome? You should draw your own conclusions. It took me years of experiencing and gathering my own evidence before I could properly decide for myself, and I certainly would not wish anyone to make the leap into deciding on this question without due consideration. It is a tremendous expansion of your consciousness to do so.

Let me give you another of my own experiences. Some time ago, a friend in London told me she was very worried about her mother, in Australia, who was supposed to have called her two days earlier but had failed to do so. When she didn't phone, my friend tried to ring her, but continually got no response. As my friend talked to me of her fears, I slowly but consciously removed myself from the sound of her voice and went into Code A. With the use of my third eye, I went to her mother's home. I described to my friend all I could see, giving as full an account as I could of everything as I moved around the home like a roving camera. Her mother wasn't there, but I sensed that she wasn't hurt and had simply gone away. Then, suddenly, an inner voice told me my friend should phone that night, when her mother would be back. She did so, and I'm pleased to say that all was well. Her mother had simply gone away for a few days – albeit that my friend was very angry with her mother for not having let her know!

FURTHER WORK WITH THE AERIAL VIEW

Once you have successfully completed the aerial view 'wake-up call' several times, you can work with it in many different ways. Don't forget to stay one step removed, like an invisible being that flies over and through buildings, with no heaviness or solidity whatsoever. Wherever you arrive is the destination, so always let it come into focus before you start to move around. If you want to be really smart, you can try viewing more difficult things such as posters, papers and documents. With experience, you will begin to sense even more than you see. Eventually, you will learn to translate what you sense to the extent that you will hear sounds and even whole conversations.

Here are a couple of interesting scenarios in which you can try using the aerial view:

- You are listening to someone talk about someone else and want to check the veracity of their information or impressions.

  Go into Code A, then take your eyes off the person who is talking and just gaze away. Now direct your thought towards the person they are talking about. You will start to get visual 'clips' of them – perhaps the way they look or where they are – and then you will start to get much more. Close down. Now share the information (without adding any 'extras').

- You receive an invitation to a party, wedding or other function and want to know whether you should go.

  Go into Code A. Hold the invitation and let yourself drift off to the function. View it, listen to what is going on, sense if it is 'your kind of thing'. Close down. You will have seen enough to know whether you want to accept or not.

To be the best in this work . . .

- See and sense – do not think.
- View without attachment.
- Describe accurately – do not add details provided by your mind.
- Keep a flow – do not leave gaps.
- Stay relaxed, happy and positive – remember it's all fun.

'SEEING' AND POSITIVITY

I believe that the greatest seers throughout history have worked by using the third eye to its full potential. Thus they have gained the ability not only to see far afield but also to move about in space and to travel through time, experiencing the past at first hand and, even more excitingly, getting detailed glimpses of the future. To me, it's as if all that was, is and is to be, is stored on a memory disc that surrounds the Earth, a disc you can click onto mentally. Whether it's on fast-forward (into the future) or rewind (into the past), the most dramatic events will be most visible – it's rather like catching only the most startling moments when fast-forwarding or rewinding a video.

When it comes to 'seeing', be it past, present or future, I like to remind myself of the saying 'Like attracts like'. It all boils down to the perception you have of yourself and your life, as these will reflect and colour your view of the whole world around you, and that includes the non-physical world. If your thought processes are negative when you are working, they will naturally click onto a frequency that will give you negative visions. In the same way, if you are feeling depressed, you will find it exceedingly difficult to click onto people and not see scenes of a 'heavy', dramatic or even frightening nature. To raise your vibration, however, requires a great effort of will, so if you are feeling down, you should not try to do so too quickly. Allow yourself a week or two, depending on how low you are feeling.

Deep in your heart, possibly yet to be awakened, is a true sense of love and gratitude for being alive at this time. Without this, you cannot easily care about other beings; nor can you wholly utilise the immense power you are unlocking in this training.

If you suffer from depression, and despair of ever climbing your way out, read Sheila's story below. It describes how one woman made this transition through the training outlined in this book, and will give you the encouragement you need. If, on the other hand, you are already enjoying the excitement of all of the new experiences the training is bringing you, please share the story with anyone you know who needs to make some crucial changes in their life.

SHEILA'S STORY: TRAINING TO ENHANCE HER LIFE

Sheila was in her late forties. She was very attractive, intelligent, always smartly dressed and had a dry sense of humour. She came from a strict but privileged background and had mixed in high society in London. She had travelled the world and had recently said goodbye to a successful career in PR.

I first met Sheila when she came to me for a sitting. A few days later she called to ask if I would train her. She told me she had been intrigued and impressed by the accuracy of what I had said in her sitting and that she now saw this work as her future pathway in life. She wanted to learn to be both a psychic and a healer. Her dream was to heal people – especially children – in mind and body.

I love Sheila. Her very down-to-earth, in-your-face way of speaking makes me laugh. There's no offence intended really, although some people would probably find her just too outspoken in her manner. Of course, it is always healthy to question, and, boy, did Sheila question!

Despite all of which, at the time I met her, she had low self-esteem – as a result of which she tended to make judgements about others continually. I have found that the more critical people are of those around them, the more they need to work on themselves. The truth is that we cannot change another's actions, only our own reaction to them, so we have to learn to live and let live. So it was vital for me to assist Sheila in discovering who she truly was and what her strengths and weaknesses really were. She had to heal wounds from her past, understand her reactions and then forgive all those involved by letting them be and allowing them to continue on their own journeys. In doing this, she would alter the trip-switch that had, up until then, always triggered verbal outbursts.

Sheila put a lot of effort into achieving this shift. She succeeded in creating a boundary around her that enabled her to choose to stop hearing others when their words were triggering her in an inappropriate way. In effect, she stopped making it personal. Once she had succeeded in doing this, she made great progress in psychic work, training with me in a small group over a number of years. In Sheila's own words, the experience 'changed my life'.

Eventually, however, she decided to pursue a more ortho-dox training alongside her psychic work. She felt that she needed this to assist and support her new-found self-esteem – it was her way of feeling credible out in the world. I could only applaud her for finally arriving at a place of wisdom and self-knowledge where she was able to discern what she truly needed.

She went on to train in craniosacral therapy in both the UK and the USA. She now uses her psychic abilities openly and courageously in her therapy work. For her, the mixture is a very happy one.

QUIZ: **HOW POSITIVE ARE YOU?**

This quiz will help you to assess how positive you are in your approach to life and to pinpoint areas where you need to do some work to cultivate self-esteem. Your responses will guide you to particular affirmations on page 158. Please answer the questions honestly!

1. For what percentage of time are you
    positive during the day or week?   .... % out of 100

2. Can you think of a past moment that
    made you laugh?   YES .... NO ....

3. Do you make judgements about
    people you know?   YES .... NO ....

4. Do you feel that society, friends or
    family owe you something?   YES .... NO ....

5. Have you ever felt great when dressed
    for a special occasion?   YES .... NO ....

6. Do you have any like-minded friends?   YES .... NO ....

7. Do you blame a family member(s) for
    the way you are in life?   YES .... NO ....

8. Do you often feel pangs of jealousy,
    for example of friends or siblings?   YES .... NO ....

9. Do you find it hard to mix socially?   YES .... NO ....

10. Are you in charge of your life?   YES .... NO ....

Now let's look at how you did. Remember, it isn't a competition. There are no wrong answers, just truthful ones. You are looking for information to help you improve your self-esteem and become the best psychic you can possibly be.

Question 1

If you answered:

Over 70 per cent Great. Keep smiling. You love yourself, and you attract people to you through giving and receiving. Keep empathy and ego in fine balance.

60–70 per cent You need to work on your self-belief. Your sense of well-being is good, but you may suffer minor ailments, such as colds, when that missing 40 per cent allows your immune system to become depleted. Stop looking for evidence of your own self-worth outside yourself. Do affirmation E.

50–59 per cent Your self-esteem is a little on the low side. You need to do more work on yourself. Drop any attachment to outcomes, both at work and socially. Do affirmation D.

Under 50 per cent You allow yourself to exist in the negative zone for far too much of your life. Self-worth, self-belief and love have been missing for too long! Gratitude for living is important – life's worth it. Do affirmation A.

Question 2

If you answered:

Yes Good. Use memories like this to boost your mood when you feel down or have negative thoughts. Do affirmation E.

No Come on! Try watching a comedy programme on TV – and laugh. Don't take yourself and life so seriously. Do affirmation A.

Question 3

If you answered:

Yes   OK, it's easy to do, isn't it? But every time you make a judgement, it reflects back on you and blocks you in looking at your personal life and issues. You are acting like a slave to your belief system – your subconscious judges. You probably also hate being criticised. Do affirmation B.

No   You have found love – for life, living and others – with no conditions attached.

Question 4

If you answered:

Yes   You have a problem! It's time to find your soul and ask why you came here. It takes energy to live and you have to increase yours. Rewards come in many guises. Self-effort is required. You can't do this on the backs of others.
Do affirmation A.

No   Great. Build up your self-esteem and start creating your dream.

Question 5

If you answered:

Yes   Yes, yes! Always enjoy your appearance – how you look shows how you feel.

No   OK, so you don't like special occasions. You don't feel good about yourself, or perhaps you don't enjoy the company of other people. It's time to recognise your good points instead. Do affirmation C.

Question 6

If you answered:

Yes   Good news. Such friends boost your energy field.

No   You can have such friends, if you wish for them. Do affirmation A.

Question 7

If you answered:

Yes   Did you answer yes to question number three? Stop and give it some thought. You have the problem. Do affirmation B.

No   You are your own person – enjoy.

Question 8

If you answered:

Yes   It's healthy to admit it, but not good to harbour such feelings. Why haven't you got what they have? Start the shift in your life. Do affirmation D.

No   You prefer inspiration to jealousy. You are on track.

Question 9

If you answered:

Yes   A big-time shift is required. You need a feel-good factor in your life. Do affirmation D.

No   Enjoy! But don't do all the talking yourself.

Question 10

If you answered:

Yes   The best! This is the greatest understanding of your life's journey.

No   Stop thinking this way. Your mind is your mind, your thoughts are your thoughts, and your wishes are your wishes. Nobody can own them but you. You need to build up your self-esteem and create a positive energy flow. Do affirmation C.

Affirmations

These affirmations are designed to change your thinking. They really can make a difference to your life. Do them first thing in the morning and last thing at night for two weeks. Look in the mirror or close your eyes, then say the words out loud. When you have finished, take a breath and smile.

If you ever find yourself backsliding, do the appropriate affirmation exercise again.

A   This affirmation will help you to be grateful.

'I thank you for the sun, my life and all that I have around me.'

B   This affirmation will help you to boost your mental and physical energy.

'I have love deep in my heart; it increases every moment I live.'

C   This affirmation will help you to realise all that you are.

'I am the power, I am in control of my life, I am safe.'

D   This affirmation will help you to make a shift.

'This is the first day of the rest of my life; I am worthy and I trust without condition.'

E   This affirmation will help you to live your dream.

'I am now living my wish in this moment and all is well in my life.'

As I have already mentioned, you cannot change a person's actions, only your reactions to them. These affirmations help you to change your attitudes and perceptions. Believe in them. You'll be amazed how differently everyone acts towards you.

THREE DAYS

Imagine for a moment that your life lasts for three days:

- **Day one** (yesterday)
  You sat and planned all you want to experience in this three-day existence for your own spiritual progress, including an order of events. You are now given the power to enact what you have chosen.

- **Day two** (today)
  You are living and experiencing the journey you have planned.

- **Day three** (tomorrow)
  You have now completed all you set out to achieve. WOW! Was that a trip!

You may now be thinking, 'But I didn't really get the house/car/relationship I wanted.' If so, I'm afraid you have missed the point! The truth is that you chose everything you needed – every event, every encounter – in perfect order, to learn for yourself and speed your progression. This is equally as true of unsettling or unnerving experiences as it is of self-evidently rewarding ones.

PSYCHIC TAKEAWAY: **THE GOLDEN LINE**

The golden line is all about creating your own personal boundary fence, the golden perimeter that surrounds your person. In psychic work, it is vital for your sanity and protection that you stay safe from anyone who – wittingly or unwittingly – 'sucks' at your energy field. This will help you to stay one step removed from any unpleasant situation, such as a verbal or physical assault. A friend who is emotionally upset or worried, a family member who is angry and sounds off at you . . . such people will all sap your energy. And if they happen over the phone, such encounters can be even more draining, because the phone piece against your ear allows a direct hit on an emotional level. Think about it. When you receive a call giving you sad news, where does it hit you physically? In the solar plexus region (below the chest) – you'll find yourself holding that place because of the anguish created by what you have heard.

So whenever anyone starts a verbal 'onslaught' (in effect offloading on you their subconscious chattering), hold yourself still for a moment, create a golden line in your mind and throw it out about a metre in front of you, completely surrounding you if necessary. And smile. You can now afford to listen and even help – without any attachment to the outcome.

Similarly, before you take that 'serious' phone call, tell yourself, 'I will not hear this.' Then you can listen and respond without taking it all on board. It's so much healthier to stay one step removed in all situations.

TESTING, TESTING, ANYBODY THERE?

The more tools and equipment you use, the less effort you allow to utilise your power. By this stage in your training, you will have created a balance within yourself and mastered the relaxation and self-healing techniques. You will have become expert at using the protocols to go into Code A and know how to act as a kind of psychic radio receiver and built-in camera. You will have learnt how to pass your messages on directly, exactly as you hear and see them. You will probably also have found out which methods of working suit you best and realised where you should focus your energy. And you will have started to experience real, positive and significant change in your life, both at work and at home. All of this is progress, so congratulate yourself on a great achievement. From now on you can really begin to work your psychic power.

The most common problem people have at this stage in the training is finding the time to continue the exercises and develop their skills. This may particularly be the case if you live and work in a city and have children. So at this point it's well worth sitting down and giving some thought to the way your life was, how it is now and how you wish it to be from now on. This may mean making some changes to your routine in order to create time and space to allow the shift to take place fully.

Of course, if you don't want to change your lifestyle, it's possible to keep your psychic ability hush-hush; however, this will effectively block any further development. One of my motivations in writing this book was to provide a resource for anyone and everyone wishing to enhance their lives by learning some basic mind techniques to empower themselves and those around them. Each step you have taken will have given you more evidence of your growing psychic ability – an ability that is way beyond the norm. I'm afraid that using your power properly doesn't allow for hiding. Nor does it allow for stagnation. So while you can listen as much as you like to other people telling you how good psychic exercises are for them, that isn't the same as doing the work yourself. That said, psychic work should always be fun and enjoyable. It should feed your inner being, make you feel good and give you a lovely warm sense of well-being.

 WAKE-UP CALL: **THE PSYCHIC PARTY**

Practising your psychic skills on friends and family will have given your confidence a great boost. Now it's time to go public and test yourself a little more by having your own psychic party, at which you offer sittings. I suggest you get everyone to chip in (parties can be costly, even if you only invite 10 to 20 people), but if you know someone who's already got a party planned, you could offer your services to them instead – on the understanding that everyone knows you are testing your ability only.

If this is your first time (so to speak) and you are nervous, my advice is that you do not give the party any thought until the actual day. Do not allow any 'what ifs' to enter your mind. Simply trust and go with the flow, telling yourself that all will be well.

On the day, wear clothes that are comfortable, with some colour – greatly beneficial to enhance your mood – and make sure you drink only water (no alcohol) while you are working. Remember never to make judgements based on the way a person looks – try to keep your gaze to one side. Always remember that the message you pass on is confidential. Never blab about what you have told your sitters. Once it has been given, only they can share the information – if they want to. Finally, don't forget to tune in and tune out with each person. I wish you an exciting and learning-filled journey.

- Before everyone arrives, find a quiet spot where you can work during the party, preferably in a separate room with two chairs and a small table.

- When you are ready – and you should be the one to decide when this is – start the sittings by greeting the first person with a smile and touching them once lightly (this aids the connection). Ask them their first name only and introduce yourself. Ask them to say nothing except 'yes' or 'no' until the sitting ends.

- Use the protocols to go into Code A (see page 97) and then begin. Tell the person everything you see, hear and feel. Don't try to make any sense out of it, just let it flow.

- When there is no more to tell, stop and use the protocols to close down. Tell the person that you have finished. I recommend that you don't allow any questions at first. Later, when you are more confident, you can give the sitter some time towards the end of the sitting to ask any questions. However, I find it best to restrict people to a maximum of three questions, otherwise the sitting will take too long and other people won't get a turn. Believe me, when people know what you're doing you'll be inundated!

- Ask the sitter what they can confirm in the message you passed on. Make a note of what they tell you. If you have given them information regarding the future, ask them to let you know if it proves correct.

- As soon as you can after the sittings are over, use your notes to complete the progress sheet on page 164.

PROGRESS SHEET

Definitions

A hit   You were spot on with what you relayed.

A miss   Your past/present names and descriptions were not
            recognised.

To come   Information that will be proved accurate or otherwise in the
            future.

Sitter's name: _____

Details that you passed on	Hit / Miss / To come
1. _____	___ / ___ / ___
2. _____	___ / ___ / ___
3. _____	___ / ___ / ___
4. _____	___ / ___ / ___
5. _____	___ / ___ / ___
6. _____	___ / ___ / ___
7. _____	___ / ___ / ___
8. _____	___ / ___ / ___
9. _____	___ / ___ / ___
10. _____	___ / ___ / ___

It is only after the event that you can give thought to and absorb what
took place and learn from it but, whatever information you got, you
deserve a big 'feel-good factor' for all the effort you put in, so
congratulate yourself. It's a great achievement to have come this far –
and if you feel the need, you can always go back to basics for a refresher.

SPIRIT GUIDES AND MESSAGES

By now you may have noticed that message techniques vary depending on who is transmitting to you. In this way, you can quickly understand whether the message is coming to you from your own spirit guide or from another spirit. Spirit guides make themselves known sooner rather than later, even if only through a sense that you are not alone, so you may not yet be fully aware who 'he', 'she' or 'they' are. Don't worry if at first most messages come through with the help of your spirit guide. In my experience, spirit guides are the most incredible teachers – but learning from them is not like going to school! They bond with you and with your energy field and are always compatible. They are understanding and compassionate – they don't have attitude, character issues, mood-swings, fits of pique, temper or any kind of bias. That was all in the past for them. All guides are in service having attained the status of the most incredible giving, forgiving and pure selflessness.

GIVING MESSAGES TO PEOPLE YOU DON'T KNOW

People I train often ask what they should do if they suddenly get a message for someone they don't know – for instance someone they are standing next to at the bus stop or meet at the office photocopier. The answer is, again, trust. It is not your job to decide when or where messages come through. Spirit people can pick up on you wherever you are, and if they need to give a message to a living loved one, they will use whatever opportunity presents itself. It is your job to be the messenger only. You cannot judge the wrong or the right of it, or the relevance of the time. Understand that whoever you give the message to will be ready to hear it, otherwise you would not be receiving it from the spirit world.

So create the moment and then pass the message on, no more no less. Once you have given the message to the person, move some distance away, with no excuses and no more words. I have found when you give a message in these circumstances it does usually create a strong reaction in the recipient. If you can touch the person gently on the arm first, it helps to make a connection and generate a positive feeling towards you personally.

I once gave a message to a girl queuing for a coffee in an office corridor. I then stepped back and moved a good distance away from her. After five minutes or so, she came to find me. She was crying and her arms were wrapped tightly around her chest. She asked me if I'd understood the message. I said no, which was true. She told me the message had been from her father. (I had given her his name.) He had passed over only the week before. Quite wonderfully, the one thing that he could have said to help her family – indeed all that they really needed to know – was contained in that message. I felt the tears start in my own eyes as the girl told me this, but they turned to tears of joy as smiles took over between us.

WHICH SPIRIT PEOPLE WILL MAKE CONTACT AND THROUGH WHOM

Not all spirit people will make contact through a medium. It takes them tremendous energy to communicate, and the experience can be as emotional for them as it often is for the recipient of the message. For these reasons some spirit people prefer to go through a third party, i.e. another spirit more used to working in this way. However, even spirits who communicate with the human world regularly may have difficulty in getting their point across to a medium. Nevertheless, with time and effort it usually gets through.

Spirit people can have similar problems to the living when it comes to communicating messages via a stranger, but generally they will try every possible means to get the message across and provide evidence of its credibility.

Spirit people are choosy about which medium they communicate through. A girl I knew called Maggie, who worked near my home, had recently lost her brother. She was considering coming to me for a sitting but needed time to build up her courage. In the meanwhile she went to Scotland to stay with her best friend for a holiday. As a treat, her friend booked an appointment with a very well known medium in Edinburgh.

Later Maggie told me she was sitting nervously waiting for a message from her brother when the medium looked up and said, 'I'm sorry, I have your brother Peter here, but he says he won't talk to me – he'll only speak through Angie!'

So never promise you can make contact with a specific spirit 'person', whether it's a sitter's long-lost friend or a loved one. You can only say you will try. Explain that you are giving a service and that it is at the spirits' bidding not yours. Sometimes you will feel pressure from the spirit person to connect before you have even tuned into Code A, as some will be there ready and waiting to go to work. You simply have to leave it up to the spirit. However, if no spirit family members or loved ones of the sitter are forthcoming, then your own spirit guide will be there to assist and act as a third party.

Once again, let me reiterate, whatever you receive – be it through vision, hearing or feeling – pass it on straightaway and quickly move on. I have to admit I learnt this in what my grand-parents would have called 'the hard way'. When I first started giving readings, in the days before I fully understood Code A, I judged a message given to me through hearing and altered it so that it made sense to me before I relayed it. Oh, whoops, never again! My spirit teachers told me that was a lesson well learnt.

GETTING MESSAGES FOR YOURSELF

I have heard and read of many psychics who say they cannot use this work to assist themselves in their own lives. However, this has not been my experience. When it comes to personal questions I have found that it is possible to receive answers from your spirit guide. These come in one of several ways. They may appear in your mind during a moment of relaxation when you have naturally slipped into Code A. They may be given to you out of the blue by an unsuspecting third party. They may come in the form of something written on a paper or in a book.

It is human nature to want proof from outside ourselves. Psychics are no exception to this rule, and so they tend to go to other psychics for their own confirmation. Being able to 'do it yourself' boils down to trust and to a tremendous amount of belief in your own ability – which can only be gained over time, from all the evidence you gather through receiving and transmitting. Clients often give feedback and this can greatly boost your confidence – though hopefully not your ego.

Ask yourself the following questions:

- Do you believe spirit people are there for you?
- Has your life changed for the better since you started this work?
- Have you had accurate visions?
- Have you successfully given proof of the veracity of your messages to those around you?
- Do you feel the power of the energy within?
- Do you believe there is a continuum after physical death?

If you can answer 'yes' to all these questions but you still cannot receive personal information from the spirits, there can only be one thing stopping you: your own personal blocking system in your mind! To overcome it, give yourself plenty of inspirational moments (see the 'psychic takeaway' on page 34) and when you truly wish to know something go straight into Code A and put the question out there on the 'net'. Then close down and allow the answer to come to you. It will arrive when you least expect it, but it will come – and when it does, remember once again not to be attached to the outcome.

PAT'S STORY

Pat was very glamorous. She had a powerful voice, a good sense of humour and a driving determination. When younger, she had been a chronic drug addict but had rehabilitated herself success-fully. She had moved to the UK from Australia after a failed marriage and, determined to pick herself up and start again, had been using her creative abilities in running a restaurant.

Pat came to visit me fully determined to become a medium. She told me she had always known she had psychic ability, and now that she had the time to do it she wanted to learn how to become a medium so she could help other people. She said that everything in her life up to then had led her to this moment – meeting with me and learning the work. She clearly had a strong and positive energy field, but she needed – and wanted – to learn how to control it. This was essential if she was to tune her mind to psychic development and so maximise her full potential.

Pat put a lot of effort into her training and practised on many friends. This not only enhanced her life and self-worth, but also greatly improved her love life! She now leads a very spiritually attuned life, working professionally as a psychic and as a healer. In her spare time she creates and sells the most magnificent spiritual paintings.

Please don't think this is a 'happily ever after' scenario. It isn't. Pat chose a very bumpy ride in life, and all credit to her for doing so. She has had her ups and downs, and has experienced many deep-rooted problems, some of which she has worked through but others of which she has yet to overcome. So, being a sensitive out there in the real world, she regularly has to go back to basics, putting herself through simple balancing and self-healing exercises whenever she feels shaky or uncertain. But at times when she hits one of these patches I always remind her that she is never alone, which now she knows.

WORKING AS A PROFESSIONAL PSYCHIC

You may decide that the self-empowerment techniques you have learnt so far have enriched your life both at home and work and that that is enough. They will certainly have rubbed off on all those around you, which can in itself be gratifying enough. However, having come this far you may wish to take an even bigger leap at some point in the future – a leap from doing psychic work as your new-found favourite pastime to making it your life's work. This will almost certainly involve not only changing your occupation but also, of necessity, charging your clients for your work.

I have always said there must be a giving for the receiving. There is a value in the work you do and money is out there for all of us. It has simply taken the place of the bartering system. I would just ask you not to limit yourself by desiring money for its own sake. Sadly, it is a human failing to judge material wealth as the major if not the only yardstick of happiness and success in life, and the surest means by which we can achieve satisfaction.

But you only have to look at some of the wealthiest people in the world to see the fallacy of such a belief. You'll notice that they almost all have what I call a big 'sense of humour failure', while their appetite for yet more wealth and more possessions rages on undiminished. Some become power hungry too. With few exceptions, these people are relentlessly seeking to fill a vacuum like a bottomless pit, desperately searching for a sense of peace and enjoyment. Sadly, first class or economy class makes no difference in the quest for happiness.

So if you do decide to become a full-time psychic, charge a fair and reasonable fee for your endeavours. It is now generally understood among humanity that your worth is valued by a financial charge. Remember, no charge at all equates to no value at all for most people out there! Worse than that, there are those who will use and abuse your ability if given half a chance. So first be sure to establish an energy of positive power all around you, then work with integrity and always keep to your financial boundaries.

I suggest that a half-hour sitting is quite long enough for one client at the beginning. It's not the amount of time you give that counts but the quality of the time given. A single, simple message can change a person's life forever, and it can be passed on in an instant.

I must warn you, however, that there are some people out there who spend a great deal of their time visiting one psychic after another, as if they're on a sort of spiritual merry-go-round. Sadly, they are not seeking genuine messages and guidance in their lives, but instead feeding an emotional need to get you to carry them through their lives. Their reality will very likely be in turmoil. You will learn to recognise the signs from both the way they speak and the activity of their energy field – which you will find needs other people's energy almost continually – yours too if it can get it, so watch out! Once they have found and connected to you, such people are likely to keep ringing you up, saying they have yet another problem and wanting you to answer still more and more questions. It's not that they are looking for true answers, they just need you as their constant prop. When you come across such a client – as you almost inevitably will at some point – the best way to deal with them is to kindly but firmly tell them that you allow clients to visit you only once a year at most. Keep your boundary.

HOW FAR CAN YOU GO WITH THIS WORK?

There is a limit to how far you can go with psychism, but only the one that you put on yourself. You can be held back by your own belief system – the fears that have been instilled in you – and your lifestyle, but otherwise the power gained from this work is endless and boundless, as indeed is the afterlife.

Many people have told me that the detailed evidence of a spirit realm that they have received has dramatically altered their attitude towards death within a very short space of time. Whereas previously they had believed that death was the end, lights out, total blackness, they have now discovered a wonderful sense of calm 'knowing' that they can and will continue in the afterlife.

 PSYCHIC TAKEAWAY: **MONEY CLOUD**

To create the fulfilment of a wish, seek the higher good without a selfish motive or any shadow of negativity or harm. This can and does invoke the most powerful energy to manifest itself.

Now, just for a moment, imagine that you can see a white cloud in the distance. Now see it as a 'money cloud'. Allow it to come over you and over your life in abundance – with no limits – and smile.

EVIDENCE FROM BEYOND 10

One thing that truly assists the psychic on their journey is feedback from clients at a later stage. I have found that while some people just come and go and never give another thought to you, the messenger, others, perhaps the majority, are exceedingly generous in sharing their stories about what I predicted and what then happened. Of course, some clients may have the opportunity to visit me only once every two or even five years, but it's great when all the same they give me the feedback on the session before. That said, if a major incident takes place that I had foretold (whether positive or negative) you can bet I get a call immediately after it happens letting me know all the details! Sometimes, too, I get feedback from friends, or via a friend of a friend. This kind of feedback always make me laugh – it's like Chinese whispers, and has to be taken lightly and with a sense of humour.

In this chapter you will find several feedback stories, covering clients' predicted significant events and the actual outcome, that have been relayed to me over time. As you read them, please notice that the words used in a sitting are always very precise. They get right to the point and have no flowery elaborations whatsoever. As I've said before, this simplicity is important. And if a client interrupts the sitting or questions the words given at that moment, you'll find that the message given to you will be repeated in exactly the same manner. Don't question it and don't waver. It has been given in this precise way for a reason, and often it is only with hindsight that the wisdom of the message conveyed can be fully understood.

Now, while all this may make good sense to you, we are all human and are naturally anxious to give as much as we can to our sitters. Do not let this feeling sway you. It is vital that the wording you are given is relayed exactly as it comes, no more and no less. It may be that this particular message is all the sitter can handle at that moment, or it may be that it is a part of an overall design that has yet to be fully formed or to become manifest – least of all to you, the messenger. You are not important in this, and for whatever reason it may be, the words you are given must be the only ones you relay. Time will tell!

Which is why feedback can be so helpful. When your sitters find out the wisdom of the words they were given, so too do you. This will give you a real boost, reinforcing your trust and confidence in the words you heard. It may sound silly, but even now, after years of passing on psychic messages, in my own child-like way I am bowled over time and time again by such feedback and overjoyed every time I receive it.

So the benefits of feedback are great. It will inspire you in your journey along this powerful and positive progressive path of spiritual learning, enabling you better to assist those in both the human and the spirit world.

LINSEY: A WEDDING

Linsey was in her twenties and had been diagnosed with chronic arthritis at the age of 18. She came from a very poor family in the East End of London, where she lived with her parents. Their home had one of those outside toilets of the kind you now usually only read about in history books. If one of the family wanted a bath, they had to bring a tin tub in from the back yard. Linsey's father had been laid off work, so she had got a job as a receptionist in the West End in order to keep the family afloat financially. It was there that I met her at work.

One day, Linsey asked me for a sitting. During the session, she was told that 'that very year, in September, she would meet a man in the most unexpected circumstances – and when least expected – whom she would marry the next year, in April'. She was then told that this relationship would change her life and benefit her health, and she and her husband would have their own home and two wonderful children.

When the sitting ended, Lindsay just laughed, saying it was 'impossible' for such a 'miracle' to take place – she never had the chance to meet anyone, let alone someone as amazing-sounding as that. All she did was travel by bus and train for an hour and a half to get to work, carrying her sandwiches, and then she took the same journey home again. What could I say to make her believe otherwise? There was nothing, of course, but the huge energy rush I had received during the sitting caused me great (and silent) excitement on Linsey's behalf. All I could do was tell her to let go and trust.

What happened

One night, in September of that year, Linsey took the train home as usual, but this time it broke down. Three hours later she got off the train and waited hopefully in the pouring rain for the bus that would take her on the last leg of the journey home. An hour later she was still there, thoroughly soaked, tired and miserable. Then, out of the blue, a police car stopped. The policeman, Craig, asked her where she was heading, then offered to take her home. Needless to say, she gratefully accepted.

The following April, I was deeply touched to receive an invitation to Linsey and Craig's wedding. I wouldn't have missed it for anything. For many reasons it's become one of the greatest experiences of my life. Not only because I had never imagined what an amazing experience a true, no-holds-barred East End wedding would be, but also because I was honoured by all of the family for the message I had passed on.

It got better still. Linsey and Craig bought their own home and now have two beautiful children. Meanwhile, Linsey's arthritis has become a thing of the past.

However many weddings I've been to since as a result of the wonder of that special psychic 'advance message service', this one will always truly pull on my heart and soul.

JEN: A BIRTH

When Jen came for a sitting, she was told;

> You are soon to be pregnant and will have a beautiful baby boy. His name will be Hugo. The man who is the father is not for you and will not marry you. There is a new relationship coming in as soon as Hugo is born. You will meet socially through a friend. A good-looking, charming man whom you will really love. He is the man you will marry and you will then have another child, a daughter, and live in the countryside.

Jen was utterly shocked at the message, but luckily she had a great sense of humour, so both of us made light of it – it wasn't what she imagined at all! Nevertheless, she wanted to stay in touch so we agreed to meet for lunch every now and then.

What happened

That same year Jen became pregnant – so our lunches became far more water than wine! Hugo was born and I became his god-mother. Within a month of Hugo's birth, his father had bowed out of the relationship and Jen had met George. She married him the following spring and within a few months was pregnant again. She had a wonderful baby girl. The family now enjoy a hectic lifestyle, all happily ensconced deep in the countryside.

CLARA: A VERY BAD FEELING

Clara phoned me late on a Monday. It was the end of her first day in a new job. She told me she was working for three directors, two of whom were great, but the third one, the finance director, was very weird indeed, and she didn't think she could work with him at all. Please could I help?

I tuned in and was given the following message.

Don't worry, Clara; he won't be there. Don't ask why, just understand there is no problem; you will be fine. The job will be very good for you and will give you the experience you need before moving on to your dream work.

When I had relayed this message, I told Clara that while receiving it I had had a very bad feeling about this man, one which was making me feel ill, so I was sorry but I couldn't tell her any more, she just had to trust.

What happened

The following Friday, Clara phoned me. 'You know that guy that made you feel ill?' she said. 'He threw himself under a train this morning.'

SUE: A NEW LOVER

Sue and I had already met socially several times through a mutual friend when she booked a sitting one New Year. As requested, she kept to the rules of no chatting, but just sat down with a cup of coffee while I tuned in and started relaying what I had received.

The main message was:

> In April you are going away for a weekend, where you will meet a new man in your life. His name is Tony, and you will know the moment you meet him that he is special. He is delightful and charming. He is a doctor. He is not British. He lives in America but travels around Europe for his work giving speeches. You will often travel with him. You will spend a lot of time together in London.

After the sitting, Sue said nothing about this to me, nor to anyone else. A year came and went. Then in May of the following year, she finally phoned me to let me know what had taken place. She said that in the previous year 'nothing had happened', so she'd just put the message to the back of her mind – very wise, I thought.

What happened

In April of that year, Sue had gone on a weekend workshop – the same one that she had done in April of the previous year. This time, however, she had met a man whom she really liked, called Tony, and they had since become 'an item'. He was a medical specialist. His home was in Canada, but he travelled around Europe giving lectures to the medical profession. And Sue added, 'Guess what – he was supposed to be at the same workshop last year but at the last minute he had to cancel, so he booked for it this year instead!'

SAM: REVEALED EVIDENCE

In Sam's sitting she was told:

> Go to your mother-in-law's house. In the bedroom, go to the wardrobe. Right at the back you must look in the boot. There you will find what you need to know.

At the time Sam said nothing about the session. I always tell people that if there are any important questions they need to ask later, they can of course phone me, but I add that they should not expect me to remember anything that took place because I never hold any memory of the sessions. Sam thanked me greatly and left.

What happened

Time went by and Sam visited again. This time, before we started, she told me what had taken place since the previous sitting. Apparently she had been extremely unhappy in her marriage. She hardly saw her husband; he always said he was just 'too busy' to be at home. As a result she had felt increasingly insignificant and unloved. She had taken the message very much on board and searched the wardrobe at her mother-in-law's house. There, to her amazement, tucked into a boot at the back, were some very revealing letters, including love letters to her husband. It turned out that he had been living a double life and was planning a divorce. Greatly hurt, Sue found the courage to take all the letters to a lawyer. She ended up winning a very beneficial divorce settlement – all thanks to that evidence.

MARY: FOOTBALL CRAZY

I had been recommended to Mary as a psychic by a friend. She had to make a long journey to get to me and she was a bit frazzled on arrival, so I gave her time to relax with a cup of coffee. However, I warned her that she should talk only about impersonal subjects, such as the traffic and the weather, as it is best for the spirits as well as for the sitter not to know anything about the client before the sitting starts.

No two sittings are ever the same, but this one was particularly distinctive. Before I had even had a chance to sit down and tune in, I noticed a spirit person walking around the room, obviously very keen for me to get started, so I quickly began. In the sitting he introduced himself very clearly as John, the client's husband. One of his messages was, 'Your ring will be there when you get home.' After tuning out, I was aware that 'he' was still very much in the room and was not about to leave!

Mary, however, had already stayed too long and was by now in quite a rush to get away. But as soon as she got up 'he' started playing football – for me the whole room had become like a football pitch as he happily dribbled the ball up and down.

I had to tell Mary what I was seeing. She burst into tears and told me that her husband had been football crazy. With that 'John' blocked me in going to the door to let her out, continually repeating, 'Ask her about her eye! Go on, ask her!'

I told him it was no good – Mary was late and she had to go. I managed to get the front door open for her, but then, because 'John' hadn't stopped shouting at me and daring me, eventually I said, 'He tells me I've got to ask you about your eye.'

Mary stopped, calmly looked away and said, 'Yes, I have a glass eye.'

Now this was something I had never noticed, so natural was she in her movements, and I don't need to tell you how small I felt at that moment. In my embarrassment I scolded her husband, telling him that if it was at all possible I would have hit him. He thought that was really funny.

What happened

Mary phoned later that day. She told me that some time earlier her husband John had died and she had subsequently lost her wedding ring. She had just got home from the sitting and was standing at the kitchen table when suddenly the lost ring landed right in front of her.

TAMMY: A HOUSE SALE

Tammy was an American who came to see me one March. She was wearing a very worried look when she arrived and was desperate to blurt out her problems – but, of course, I wouldn't let her speak. I told her I didn't work that way and that she had to just sit down, keep quiet and trust what came through. If there was anything else she needed to know at the end of the sitting, at that time she could ask questions.

Two of the messages relayed in her sitting were: 'Your house will be sold by the end of May' and 'You alone will travel back to the UK in mid-July'. (This last one was repeated very clearly twice.)

What happened

A year later Tammy came to see me again. She told me that she and her husband had been trying to sell their home in the US for over a year when she first came to see me, adding that they were desperately worried about money because they couldn't sell. Laughing, she said that by the beginning of May they had both decided, 'Angela must have got that wrong, because we haven't sold yet.'

However, on 27 May cash buyers appeared. On 31 May the contract was signed. Tammy told me, 'We both thought that was pretty smart!'

Then Tammy told me she had thought I'd made an error in the last sitting when I'd said, '*You alone* will travel back to the UK in mid-July.' She had questioned the message at the time, but exactly the same words had been repeated. She had forgotten all about this until recently, when she listened to the tape of the sitting again. Apparently, both she and her husband had booked flights to come to the UK on the 17 July, but her husband had passed over suddenly with a heart attack in June, so she'd ended up coming alone, just as the message had said she would. I must admit that took my breath away, but Tammy was calm when she said, 'They knew all along, didn't they?'

JIM: THE MUSIC BIZ

'Jim' was the lead singer in a very well-known group. I am using a pseudonym here, since I am not one for knowing who's who in any business and don't want to make his identity public. His US agent knew me well and had made the appointment.

Jim didn't share with me what he got from the messages I gave. However, a year later he came back for a second sitting. This time he told me that he had been quite freaked out by what I had told him. I should let you know at this point that I always tape my sessions, and in this case Jim had personally unwrapped a brand-new tape and put it into the machine himself.

What happened

What Jim heard when he played back the tape later was the most amazing music playing in the background all the way through our session. And he loved it so much that he had written it all down and used it in his next album. How cool is that? I thought!

CREATING A BOND

There is another advantage to receiving feedback, too. It creates a bond. When you work for people – and by 'people' I mean both living clients and their nearest and dearest in the spirit dimension – in this very personal, intimate and private way, you are making a direct connection with them. You are instrumental in creating for them the very closest of links between the two worlds – human and spirit – in their ongoing lives.

To me, time and money are of little or no consequence when set against the rewards of love and warmth that can and will come when you are doing this work properly. As I share the encounters described in this chapter with you now, I feel a tremendous glow that makes me smile – for all of them.

So I can promise you that, in no time at all, you will be giving out a message that, while it may seem very short and insignificant to you at the time, will touch the heart and soul of the recipient sitting opposite you. And in return you will feel the love and warmth that it brings, for you are the intermediary, the single, vital link that makes it all possible.

PSYCHIC TAKEAWAY: **HELP**

Help comes in strange ways, often in that moment when least questioned and a delightful surprise. As soon as you open the window of trust, in comes help. You have only to stand and wait in one place for a few seconds and help will appear beside you. Help draws you to the place ahead and shows you where to look – where to go and where to seek. Even where to look for that lost item.

TAKING THE JOURNEY 11

In case you are wondering, you are not alone in what you're now going through! It's human nature to want to identify with those who have had similar experiences to your own, so let me reassure you: the experiences you have had, are having and are yet to encounter have all happened and are all still happening to someone else in the psychic field already.

DON'T LOOK BACK

If you have been addicted (be it to drugs, alcohol, sex, gambling or anything else) and you have done your time in rehab, then you know that what you need right now is to create a new lifestyle – with support – and move ahead. Never look back. The work of building your self-esteem, self-worth and self-love is paramount, as is knowing the trip-switches that led you down that terrible path in the first place.

If you should happen to be in therapy as you are reading this, just remind yourself that there is a time for its completion – and only you will know when that is. When that time arrives and the therapy sessions are no more, as with any empty space, you will need something positive to take its place. As I have already said, you should never leave a void. If you have decided to follow the psychic path, you will probably feel the need for some support during the early stages. I would therefore suggest that you work with a spiritual group or circle; go to one of the many specialist colleges for training; or use any of the psychic tools you feel drawn to, such as the Tarot.

Should you find that you wish to become a healer, you have a choice between training with a spiritualist group such as the National Federation of Spiritual Healers (NFSH – see the Resources section on page 235 for further details) and going on to work purely as a spiritual healer, or training as a counsellor or complementary therapist and using your psychic abilities to enhance this work. The field is open and the choice is yours.

Then again, perhaps you already have a career and simply wish to enrich your life with psychic work. While there's no doubt that psychism can greatly benefit you in your work, I have a caveat to issue here. If you are a very good psychic (which I expect you now to be) and your present work doesn't involve helping people, there will surely come a moment when you feel yourself compelled to shift to a more rewarding occupation that involves giving service to others.

Bold as it may seem, be sure to make that move. Just do it.

CONTINUING TO DEVELOP YOUR PSYCHIC ABILITIES

When you have completed the training in this book, you may want to continue your psychic development, advancing further or learning another psychic skill. The following are some of the ways in which you can proceed:

- If you would like to learn Tarot, palmistry, astrology or graphology (deciphering handwriting), there are numerous colleges that teach these subjects. At most of them you can register to do a part-time course spread over one or two years. See the Resources section on page 235, search on the internet or scan advertisements in the psychic press (see the Resources on page 236). Alternatively, pick up a book that just 'feels' right for you and study it in your own time at home. If you love to surf, there are many sites and innumerable pages on all of the above subjects and more. Often they offer training as well – or at least point you in the direction where you will find it.

- Try joining a psychic development circle (see below for more information on these). Some of the specialist magazines, such as *The Psychic News* (see the Resources section on page 236) have listings of circles all over the country, area by area. (What's also great about this newspaper is that it will keep you up to date with all the latest psychic goings-on.) Alternatively, you could try starting your own psychic development circle with like-minded people. From then on it's up to you. You can make as much or as little of the circle as you wish, working on a variety of different techniques. You can also try different circles and move on when you are ready. For more information on starting your own circle, see page 192.

- If this training is your first experience of doing psychic work, I suggest that you search for a psychic mentor. Although having completed all the 'wake-up calls' successfully, you should be really pleased with yourself, it is extremely valuable to have someone to guide you and help you along further. This might be someone who is already running a circle or – if you have like-minded friends who would also like guidance – would be prepared to do so. Ask for the right mentor to come into your life and then follow your senses. You will know when you find the right one.

There are also several psychic/spiritual magazines on the newsagent's shelves (and many more on the paranormal), which you can browse through to find centres and individuals offering their services in all aspects of psychic work. Psychism is a world-wide phenomenon, so it doesn't matter which country you live in, you will find the information you seek – and don't forget the internet, which is great for bridging distances.

PSYCHIC CIRCLES

A psychic circle is simply a group of like-minded people who get together in order to develop or use their psychic abilities. There are two basic types of circle, a development circle and a spirit circle. These are described below.

Development circles

As the name suggests, this kind of circle is all about developing your psychic skills. You can use all of the exercises in this book as your training module. Spread the 'term' out over a few months, meeting say once a fortnight, to allow time for everyone to absorb the learning and for each individual's experiences to become part of their progressive development. The person who runs the training should be a natural leader, someone who exudes positive energy, has a warm and generous nature, is a good organiser and doesn't take themselves too seriously.

Spirit circles

The idea of a spirit circle is not only to develop your psychic ability to hear, see and feel spirit people, but also to encourage you to go with the flow through trust. This type of circle should be led by an experienced medium with all the qualities of a natural leader outlined above. They should be able to act as a proper, responsible mentor to all members of the group.

In the circle, the medium should always use relaxation techniques and take the group through self-healing processes before starting any other work. Then they should lead the whole group into Code A and call in each of the group's spirit teachers or guides to help them. They should also create a protective circle of positive white light around the whole circle. This links the group's energy fields tightly together for the time the circle is open, greatly boosting the overall power, energy and protection available.

The medium should then direct the group to seek messages from their spirit guides, ask for answers to any questions they have and pass on psychic messages they have received for other group members. They should also cover any of the many areas of spiritual learning that the group are ready for. The idea is to strengthen any areas of weakness the members may have and help them to become the best they can possibly be at what they do. The group should be encouraged to work with clarity, to be specific in the messages they receive and, above all, to trust their results.

No one should leave the circle until the medium has properly closed it down, as this can undo the protection put in place at the start. Be aware of this if you yourself run a circle. You must close circle, by saying out loud:

> I now close this circle and thank all our guides for their help and assistance.

Then lead everyone out of Code A.

At this point I must add another word of warning, one that seldom gets a mention. If anyone in the group has an ailment, however minor, at the time the circle is opened, that ailment can be spread among the other members. This is because you are all sharing your etheric fields, so any illness – even one that is not infectious in physical terms – can attach itself to everyone else's etheric layer and bury itself in their physical body.

In my early days as a medium, I was once running a circle for five people. Unfortunately, I had forgotten to tell the group that they should let me know if they had any medical problems. It turned out that one of them, let's call her Jane, indeed did. After the circle we all went home and by early evening I had become dreadfully aware that I was suffering from the onset of piles – or *haemorrhoids*, for the hard of hearing. I then received three somewhat awkward calls in quick succession from other group members all telling me they had the same thing! Now, I may be slow sometimes, but I quickly did the maths and phoned the remaining two. And, yes, we all had piles!

To her credit (and embarrassment), Jane admitted that she had had this problem for a number of days. She was shocked when I told her she had shared it with all of us. However, we laughed a lot, and as a result I have a learning experience that I share with every new group I lead – well before I open the circle.

Starting your own circle

It may be that you've worked through this book once already and are using it again as a booster and refresher course. In this case, you may feel that you are ready to set up your own development circle. By this stage, there will probably be many like-minded people around you who will be keen to join.

Once your circle is set up, as I mentioned earlier, it is advisable to arrange it for one evening every fortnight, or even once a month. After a period of some weeks, create a break, rather like school holidays. This gives people time to live the psychic lifestyle, go through psychic encounters and steadily progress at their own speed. It is amazing what experiences people recount on their return, as you will find out.

The idea is to be varied in the learning you undertake and to make it as much fun as possible – everything in this book is enjoyable for a group to do. With this in mind, the following are responses to a set of questions I asked the group I work with in circle presently. They should give you some idea of the many different needs and expectations people have, as well as the equally different things they get out of being in the group. Despite these differences, the circle runs extremely well. We always end up laughing a lot and having a great deal of fun.

Question 1: What made you decide to join the circle?

Kate: I wanted to further my spiritual life with like-minded people who could help me progress and who could understand.

Andrew: Curiosity and a wish to develop spiritually.

Richard: I was looking for answers to my questions.

Sarah: A strange happening in the USA linked to a local story that has no written authenticity; I believe I was led here.

John: The want and need to develop spirit communication.

Question 2: What has the circle done for you so far?

Kate: It has made me more aware of myself and of others, and helped me to understand the divine force working around us.

Andrew: Made me examine myself, my relationships, friends, aims and desires – positively.

Richard: It has introduced me to like-minded people and given me the confidence to go on.

Sarah: Made me more confident and able to deal with situations far better. Helped me to realise and develop the spiritual talent I have.

John: Increased my awareness and given me extra tools to use to further my development.

Question 3: How has it changed your life and how you see it?

Kate: It has made me more confident to walk my spiritual path, and to do it with confidence, and made me realise you are responsible for yourself.

Andrew: Made me less negative; made me realise others have the same worries, fears, anxieties and wishes that I had and have; put me in touch with another 'dimension'.

Richard: It has taught me to not judge people, to live life for today and not to worry about tomorrow.

Sarah: Helped me filter out the good and the bad people that have been or are in my life. I have become more passive and laid-back, and able to assess situations better.

John: Given me a direction and focus. Life now seems to make more sense.

Question 4: What do you expect to achieve now in the circle?

Kate: I wish to continue to improve my mediumship and be aware of the universal influences around me.

Andrew: Greater depth and understanding, and ever greater psychic and other abilities.

Richard: To be able to ask more questions and be more spiritual.

Sarah: Wish to contact spirit and hold conversations, so need to develop how I interpret the messages I receive.

John: To develop to a point with which I feel happy. To give the truth.

Question 5: How do you see this working in your life ahead?

Kate: As my spiritual ability improves, I not only manage to assist myself on my own path but can help others towards a more spiritual world.

Andrew: Allowing me to relax and enjoy more, to find true enjoyment and happiness.

Richard: To be able to help others with the same interest.

Sarah: This will help immensely with the work I wish to move on to, in which it will benefit animals spiritually.

John: Hopefully to carry out more spiritual work and to be able to give accurate and true spirit communication.

I can only repeat that it is your own journey, one hopefully made with the wish to progress and not flounder. So always endeavour to have an interest in the people you are serving, and use your skills with humility. You really don't have to become something in the eyes of others, only something in your own, so forget the ego, it has no place.

PLATEAUS

It is easy to become disillusioned when you plateau at various stages in your psychic life. You should be aware that this happens to all of us at one time or another and is simply part of the learning process. It is vital to allow yourself time to digest and assimilate what you have learnt during the training. So relax, be cool and remember you can't enjoy the ups without the downs and a few in-betweens along the way.

WAKE-UP CALL: **CHECK IT OUT**

In this exercise, you will use a social situation to practise picking up on what people are thinking. You can also try it at work or at college. Make sure you ask people first if they are happy for you to try – tell them it is all part of your training. This exercise is a great test of your ability.

- Once you have asked permission from your chosen person, use the protocols to go into Code A (see page 97). Make sure you are in a positive mood by giving yourself an inspirational moment (see the 'psychic takeaway' on page 34).

- Now see if you can pick up on the person's thoughts. Use the following questions to guide you:
  – How are they feeling?
  – What is on their mind?
  – Where do they live?
  – What have they just been doing?
  – What are they planning to do next?
  Don't overdo it; keep it simple.

- When you have finished, use the protocols to tune out (see page 97) and then check what you received with the person.

A DAY IN THE 12
LIFE OF . . .

So you are ready to take that final big step. By now you will have practised on your family and your friends, done a few psychic parties and improved each time. Now, eager or not, it's time to face the outside world. But what messages will you get for a complete stranger, one who is ready to trust you with their innermost questions and is paying you money to give them answers? Will you land on solid ground after you step off?

Have faith – your training and your guides will not desert you.

Whatever comes through your door from now on in your journey will only be ever more surprising. In this chapter I offer you a few examples of the variety of different experiences you may encounter, in this case my own.

OUT-OF-BODY PROOF

My husband and I were at a dinner party. The hostess, Georgina, told me she really wanted to believe there was something in this 'psychic spiritual stuff' but couldn't because, as she said, 'I've never seen any proof of it for myself.' I laughed and replied:

> That's such a bummer, isn't it? I mean it's all right for me, I have my proof, but it seems to you that you will never know. Why don't you ask for proof? If you're ready for it, you'll get it I'm sure.

That night Georgina got into bed and was just dropping off to sleep when she was suddenly aware there was someone in her room. She sat up to see me standing there (clothed, I might add) giving her a knowing smile. She was shocked but not frightened (as she knew it was me) and leapt out of bed, whereupon I disappeared through the wall. She spent the next few hours sitting up with a stiff drink!

A TELEPATHY TWIN THING

For my twin and me, Christmas was always a big celebration for family and friends. You know how it is – lots of presents around a tree all lit up and decked ready for Christmas Day.

Every Christmas my twin had failed to keep what she'd bought me a secret, and this one was no exception. It was just after midnight on Christmas Eve when I decided to take the dogs out and check on the horses. As I turned off the stable lights and came back through the gate towards the house, I was aware that I wasn't alone. Then I heard my twin, as though she was there right beside me, speak to me using my nickname: 'Geela, do you want to know what you've got for Christmas – in that big box under the tree?' As usual I couldn't resist and so replied, 'Go on, what is it?' With great glee she said, 'It's a scanner for your computer!' I smiled, having fallen for it once again.

But this time it was different. My twin, Engie, had passed over the year before. I was elated that she'd kept her promise to communicate, and I wasn't surprised, but I was delighted, when I opened the big box on Christmas Day to find it contained a scanner from my stepfather.

VISION IN ADVANCE

A friend and her son, Jed, were staying with us in Wiltshire. All day Jed had been messing around and testing my patience, to the extent that I'd threatened him with a thick ear if he carried on. It was a summer's evening and when I jumped in my car to collect my sister from the nearby train station, to no one's surprise a still boisterous Jed said he wanted to come with me. So off we both went.

The station was in a rural spot, so when I eventually pulled out of the car park I was shocked when an alarming vision flashed full-on in front of my eyes: a green car was in front of me and seconds later I would smash right into it, even though there was nothing else on the road at the time.

The vision had such an impact on me that I told my sister about it and then drove extra slowly for the next two miles up the lane. At the junction with the main road, I stopped and waited patiently behind another car, both of us signalling to turn left. To the right (the way we were looking to check) there was a long gap, with no cars coming.

Then the green car ahead accelerated out of the junction and I did the same, following it – but the driver ahead must have lost his nerve halfway out because he suddenly stopped dead in the road.

I drove straight in to him at 0–60 in a second! Fortunately, the worst thing that happened was that Jed hit his left ear on the front headrest, ending up with an enormous thick ear!

NUMBER SYNCHRONICITY

A clairvoyant I knew in Brighton had told me once that he could see the mark of the number four in my hand, which I found most amusing – with as many lines there as I have you could see almost anything you wanted to! But he insisted that four would be a very significant number for me personally at some time in the future, as would the numbers 13 and 31, both adding up to four. He said it could be something to do with the Lottery but it could also be to do with dates, such as 13 April. OK, I thought. We'll see.

Some time later, a very special auction was announced. It was to be the first time in history that Lipizzaner horses (the white leaping horses from Vienna) would be sold in the UK. My childhood dream had been to own one of these. Of course, I had no money – just the dream.

Kate, a very close friend who worked with me (you have read about her on page 122), went with me to visit the stud. I just couldn't stop myself going to look. There were many pens but there was only one I was drawn to – full of foals. I stood still among them until one – and only one – foal came up to me, and that was that! She was the one I wanted (or who wanted me). I promptly nicknamed her Lipi. Later, the manager gave me her full details and off we went to the auctioneers to register a bid. I had no idea of a price or reserve and, as I said, I had no money, only my immense excitement and my dream.

One week before the auction, a major client of mine telephoned, asking me if I would run a party at his house in London to celebrate the completion of his forthcoming film. Thinking of Lipi, I asked for cash in advance, and as my client knew me well enough, he kindly agreed. Then an old friend turned up at my home: he had heard I needed some financial help and he generously offered to lend me his savings.

I put all the money in a bag, took it to the auctioneers and told them to bid for Lipi – no more than I gave them, and no less if necessary, to include VAT.

Now:

- The date of the auction was 13 April 1985.
- The date of the film party was 13 April 1985.
- The lot number for Lipi was 31.
- Lipi's date of birth was 31.5.1984.
- The auction was held four miles from my home.
- Lipi cost me a total of £1,300 to buy – the exact sum I'd given the auctioneers.

The film party was for Jim Henson (he of Muppet fame), the film was *The Labyrinth*, and I was able to tell Jim later that day that it was thanks to him that my dream had come true. He was delighted.

BURGLAR BEWARE

We were packing to go on holiday. I'd just closed my suitcase when a 'voice' calmly but authoritatively told me, 'You are going to be burgled.'

I stayed absolutely still as the exact same words – but nothing else – were repeated twice more. Seconds went by, but there was nothing more, so I said out loud, 'Well, in that case I'm going to take my favourite things with me, hide my jewellery and leave my confidential papers locked in a briefcase', all of which I then arranged.

We left for the holiday, a week went by and a friend went to our flat to water the plants. She opened the door to utter devastation – the door was smashed in and the whole place turned upside down, with things scattered everywhere. She was completely unnerved.

But the burglar never found my hidden jewellery, and my briefcase was smashed but unopened! While I did pick up the age, appearance and other details about the thief psychically, without physical evidence or a real-life witness, the police said they could do nothing more.

A GIVEN TIME

Andrew and I had decided to get married. We were both living and working in London during the week and travelling to our country retreat at weekends, where my mother and stepfather looked after my retriever dog Sophie on their farm.

One day, Andrew suggested that as we were getting married we ought to start bringing Sophie to London to get her used to the two homes. I was amenable to the idea until, the very next day, I heard a voice saying, 'No, wait until your marriage.' It was such a strong prompt that I couldn't possibly ignore it, so I told Andrew that night that we should respect the message as given. Disappointed but already familiar with my messages, he reluctantly agreed to do so.

The night before our wedding, quite suddenly Sophie became extremely ill and we had to take her straight to the vet. He did many, many tests and finally found that her digestive tract had become paralysed, but he was still unsure why. So she had to stay at the vet's, on a drip, while he tried everything he could think of to find out what had caused this terrible condition and defeat it.

The next morning – immediately before our wedding cere-mony – we went to the surgery, only to hear the worst possible news: Sophie was dying of a very rare disease that only a handful of animals throughout the world had suffered from.

We had no option but to let her go and have her put down straightaway. It was a deeply sad moment in both our lives, but I was grateful for the warning I had been given: 'No, wait until your marriage.'

A SOCIAL PSYCHIC

A friend had invited Andrew and me to a dinner party. I walked into the sitting room before dinner to find Andrew seated on a large sofa talking to an attractive female guest. They were both fully engrossed in conversation and neither noticed my presence. OK, it was a large room, but I still felt a little peeved, so I simply sat on another sofa opposite them, a coffee table in between, escorted only by my glass of wine.

I found myself listening in to what the woman was telling Andrew. She was talking about her wedding in the South of France, how her husband had bought the most amazing rock-sized diamond for her and how it had been flown down especially for their wedding. Then, quite suddenly, I was aware of a man standing to my left. He was fully apparent to me but obviously in spirit form, as he was ever so slightly translucent. He was standing by the coffee table, watching and listening to them both with his ear cocked. Frowning suddenly, he then blurted out (in inner voice): 'That's not true. Go on – ask her!' He then went on to tell me a rather different story from the woman's. I couldn't believe it. He was so definite and he was giving me a chance to interrupt as well!

So I did. 'Excuse me,' I said. 'I'm sorry, but that's not quite true, is it, what you just said?' The woman turned her head sharply towards me and asked somewhat frostily, 'What do you mean?' I repeated what I'd said, going on to describe in detail the man I could see, including what he was wearing, and telling her exactly what he had said – which was basically that the vast 'rock' hadn't arrived in time for their ceremony.

She gasped and looked really quite shocked, but she slowly composed herself, and then, regarding me with different eyes, said:

You've just described my late husband. He's the only person who could have known that . . . No, the ring didn't turn up, so I had to use a curtain ring instead. We laughed about it lots at the time, and afterwards. He'd taken so much trouble too.

We went in to dinner, and at one point the woman started talking about her two marriages. That was when I received yet another message: 'That's a lie, she's had three – go on, ask her!' So I put down my knife and fork and interrupted her again – only I just couldn't bring myself use the word 'lie' in front of all the other guests, so instead I said, 'I'm sorry, but that isn't quite true either, is it? What about the third one?' I thought she was going to lean over and hit me, or at least get up and leave, as she suddenly looked so alarmed. Then, red-faced and horrified, she exclaimed, 'Oh my god, it's not safe for me to stay here, not at all – I keep that other marriage secret!' I had by now put my hand over my mouth to stop myself blurting anything else out, and we all quickly changed the subject.

For the record, it turned out that the woman's husband (the one who had appeared before me) was a celebrated Hollywood film director – when she finally told me who he was, I had to smile. But much as I'd love to, I cannot divulge his name – you'll just have to guess for yourself.

IT'S HER TIME

It was late one Friday night and we had just arrived back at my family home when my stepfather told me that Yo-Yo, one of our family cats, had developed a painful cyst which the vet was going to remove the next morning. I went to her and put my hands on her. By going into Code A and directing my thoughts to transmit a positive flow of healing energy through my fingers I could help relieve the pain that was obviously throbbing very heavily in her head.

Just then I heard the voice of my mother, who had passed over the year before, whisper soothingly in my ear, 'It is her time, darling.' Hearing this, I sadly and resignedly stroked Yo-Yo some more, giving her all my love, then got up and went to bed. I told Andrew about it but no more was said.

The next morning my stepfather took Yo-Yo to the vet's while I was busy with a couple of clients. It was lunchtime when he returned. Then, suddenly, he and my husband exploded into the room – where my clients were still sitting drinking their coffee. Both my stepfather and Andrew were in a terrible state. Andrew said quietly, 'Yo-Yo's dead; the vet's here and he's in tears – it seems he made a mistake and wants to apologise.'

I couldn't muster up the courage inside me to go and see him at that moment, as I first had to come to terms with the shock of what I had just heard. My clients were just finishing their coffee, so they thoughtfully got up and left. But in all fairness, how could I point the finger of blame at the poor distraught vet, knowing that I had heard, 'It is her time, darling' the night before?

DRINKS WITH JERRY SPRINGER?

We were just about to leave for dinner with our friend Johnnie when I got a call pleading with me to 'please, please make it for a drink with Jerry Springer' at a TV studio that evening. I had apparently been highly recommended by a close friend and he wanted to discuss the possibility of having me on his new UK show. I didn't take many of the very sparse details on board, but I was intrigued to meet 'the man', so on the understanding that Johnnie and Andrew would be coming with me, the meeting was agreed. It just so happened that we were going to have dinner near the venue anyway.

On arrival at the TV building, my name was taken and we were asked to take a seat. After a few minutes, a man appeared and asked if I was there for the casting. I said, 'I don't believe so – I'm not an actress.'

A moment later, he appeared again and asked me to come with him. I looked at Johnnie and Andrew and we all said, 'Let's go.' But at that the man said, 'Oh no, only you,' pointing at me. With that, I promptly sat back down again and said, 'No, it's all of us or nothing.'

He scuttled off, and a few minutes later came back to usher us into another room. There must have been more than 20 people sitting round a very long table, as well as some sort of 'audience' out in front. Spotlights were on and the cameras were rolling. Jerry and his producer were sitting at the centre of the proceedings and suddenly all eyes focused on me.

Within seconds it became one of those very awkward moments. Jerry asked, 'So what can you tell me?' and grinned. Then his producer asked, 'Tell me something about me and my past then.' Nothing felt right; indeed, it hadn't felt right from the moment we arrived. I should have just left at the very beginning, but the child within me had too much curiosity – and I love going with the flow, experiencing, absorbing and hopefully learning something new.

Although there was no way I was going into Code A in a situation like this, in which the atmosphere reeked of ridicule, cynicism and contempt, I was able to have an aerial snoop at the producer's lifestyle to date. And I was not amused by what I saw, heard or felt. There was nothing positive or polite that I could tell him, especially in front of all those people. He could afford to be blasé, as he obviously felt that all psychic work was a complete load of nonsense. So I simply said, 'Do you really want me to say what I am seeing? It's not exactly what I think you would want aired in public, as you obviously get up to some pretty "heavy" stuff.'

The producer froze, while Jerry shifted uneasily in his seat and, grinning with embarrassment, said, 'Well, you're quite right, so you certainly know him!' And with that I was thanked for my time and we left. My last words were, 'Hey, thanks for the drink, Jerry!'

LIGHTS OUT WITH JOHNNY DEPP

Once again, Andrew and I were about to go out for dinner when I received a pleading phone call from a client. Would I do her a very big favour? She was so persuasive that I found myself saying yes before I realised that she meant me to do it now. Very American!

A short while later, I found myself heading towards a major West End hotel in a taxi, still dressed in jeans and a jumper. I was met there by an extremely well organised woman, who whisked me quickly and surreptitiously upstairs to her suite. There, she asked me if I wanted to know anything about the person I was going to see, at which point I explained that it didn't make any difference to me who it was at this time of night. I was only there to help.

Next, two men arrived and whisked me quickly away again, this time up to the penthouse suite. I was already very tired and asked them their names three times as we rode up in the lift, so I'm sure they thought I was bonkers. The names just didn't register, and meant nothing to me at all at the time, so I didn't know that one of them was very famous indeed.

I arrived at the penthouse suite with the two men and gave the sitting, hardly coming up for air it seemed. With my eyes closed, I was far more in the other world than in the hotel room. All I can really remember is hearing a sharp shout and a shrill gasp at some point. When I had finished and tuned out, I opened my eyes to find the suite completely in darkness. Apparently, in the middle of proceedings the electrics had blown out across the entire floor, but no one had dared to stop me while I was rabbiting away in full flow!

So it was dark when I left the room, asking the two men to escort me and explaining that if I were on my own in the lift it could malfunction (it's too often happened to me before), leaving me stuck in there with a load of ghost people until morning! They both went very quiet and walked me down to the front door of the hotel.

The next morning I received a big thank-you phone call, in the course of which I asked who on earth I had sat for.

'You really don't know?' replied the agent with surprise. 'That was Johnny Depp . . . He said you were really great!'

WAKE-UP CALL: **LOOK TO THE FUTURE**

Now that you are able to look at both your own and the world's future, try this exercise.

You will need: A notebook and a pen.

- Use the protocols (see page 97) to go into Code A. Now transport yourself into the future and see what is happening. You might like to choose specific years, for example 2009, 2012 and 2018. You can zoom in on cities across the globe on specific dates of your choosing.

- Write down what you get in your notebook, together with the date and the time that each event will take place. Put the book away and keep it safely.

- When each date comes around, check your notebook and see how accurate your predictions were. You will be amazed at just how many were right on the mark.

TERMS AND CONDITIONS 13

Isn't it a wonder with all these things unseen,
Isn't it a wonder with all that has been,
To know just where you are,
Then to dream of life afar?
Life can only make sense when you know
Where you've come from is written where you'll go.
The experience was of your own choosing;
All is your gain not your losing,
What you suffer and inflict
Or on your self an addict.
Progress only comes through learning;
Don't let it become discerning.
Feeling lost and forlorn?
Remember, you chose to be born.
Put it right in this life
And so now drop all the strife.

Are there such things as laws of the universe? Yes, I believe there are and that they were created to safeguard our universe and all the life forms that live in it. These laws forbid humanity from destroying planet Earth, as that would in turn cause the destruction of all the other parts of the universe.

Our universe is overseen by a vast amassed 'knowing', with a depth and capacity way beyond the intelligence of humankind.

I believe that this intelligence has form and visited Earth a long time ago. It not only watches over us but will visit again. Our planet emits positive energy to the universe, but if we go into self-destruct mode (the way we have been heading for a long time now), we will negate everything. And it's no use passing the buck on to the next generation – it is now that matters. Governments are too often torn between principles and expediency and so do not abide by the universal law, preferring to be *seen* to do the right thing instead. Thus there is a political sham, with denials on a national and an international scale. Indeed, I would venture that the universal laws have not been adhered to during this civilisation or even the previous one.

But are the laws of the universe way beyond humanity's understanding? No, not if we can understand laws that have been shaped and laid down by democratic governments, created by the people for the people, with a true desire for peace and good will. I don't say this lightly. If we can create order and rules in our own home, village, town, city and state, it is not so different to accept order and rules for the world, and only one step further to envisage an order of law for the universe.

Take a moment to consider this. If you were to take yourself off planet Earth and observe all our goings-on from a distance, what laws would you create to stop the family, tribal, national and international envy, hatred and exploitation, the continual wars, the smell of burning rainforests, the stench of poisons ruining the land, and all the suffering, the cruelty and the injustice?

Well? It's a bit too much for the human mind, isn't it? So to understand where we humans fit in we have to go back to some basic principles that originated from a far deeper and greater 'knowing' than our own. It is on this level that, in a single cell, our individual DNA was stored for us, holding the memory. The whole human psyche originates from that original cell, a truth universally understood by mankind at the soul level. So, while each individual human being is allowed to develop freely at their own pace and in their own lifetime, it is the mind that generates our every thought and action, and we have ultimately to be responsible and learn to discern for ourselves. All is recorded on the spirit net.

INTELLIGENT SOURCE?

From what I have seen and experienced beyond the physical plane, I would say that, without a shadow of doubt, there is an intelligent source – one whose intelligence exceeds that of us mere mortals by far. Yet it is very difficult for the human mind to comprehend exactly what or who this intelligent source could be, let alone how it could possibly oversee such a vast universe. To call this an intelligent wisdom is the least I can do, as humanity has been allowed to survive willy-nilly without obvious divine influence. Every now and then help has been given by way of a more intelligent soul arriving direct from the source to offer their spiritual teachings. The Buddha, Mohammed and Jesus are among the ancient sages who have entered human bodies and so been able to give their teaching and guidance. At these times, at least some enlightenment comes forth, but sadly humankind is a very 'physical' being altogether, one that has become dulled by the sheer weight of its physical desires and weaknesses, to the detriment of the soul's journey.

The source of the universe has an attachment to the spirit net, and by this means information can filter through. I am also convinced from the knowledge I have gleaned so far that a great number of souls have chosen to be here 'in the living' right now in order to assist in the imminent shift of human consciousness and to help us all throughout the difficult period we have now entered.

Imagine yourself as a multi-dimensional traveller, without the need of gravity or oxygen. It is only your second body, the astral counterpart of your physical one, that is required. Then you can get a sense of the vast potential that awaits you. It seems incredible, but most human minds are blocked from even imagining the places of vast power from whence they came. It is simply too much to take on board. Nevertheless, I believe that the 'knowing' of the memory disc is in us all.

A TIME OF CONSTANT CHANGE

A fundamental principle of the universe is that nothing is permanent. All things are in a state of flux. Under the universal laws we exist, but while it is the given right of each of us to enjoy the goodness of living with a sense of peace and achievement, far too many of us continue to inflict discord. We abuse our free will by feeding extreme desire for power, greed, jealousy and fear, in turn destroying environments, animals, other people and ourselves.

While animals and all other life forms are responding as best they can to human abuse, sadly the negative behaviour of humanity is gaining in intensity all the time, spreading like a global disease, its causes and effects rippling around the planet at every level. We are creating a dense fog of negativity that we no longer can see our way through. This fog vibrates continuously around the Earth's force field in the universe and then ricochets back, making the planet ever sicker. The symptoms of this sickness are already evident, in the form of increasingly frequent freak weather patterns, earthquakes, volcanoes, tsunamis and floods on a vast scale.

This responsibility for the future healthy existence of Earth – and with it the universe – is the hardest and harshest lesson anyone can imagine calling in upon themselves. Yet, reluctant or not, in denial or not, we are here at this time to learn this lesson and get it right. It is in the hands of each and every one of us alive now to create this shift in understanding.

DEATH

However you dress it up, death is a natural process that happens to us all. And after death there is yet another natural process: passage into a dimension of unimaginably wonderful proportions encompassing all possibilities and providing for all opportunities to gain supreme and lasting happiness. All life forms have right of entry to this dimension; this right is unconditional and not restricted to any type of being. It is not dependent upon one's beliefs, faith system or anything else.

In human terms, at the moment of passing (dying) we slip out of the heavy body we have inhabited and glide through to a level that suits our thought-personality encased in an outer form shaped, desired and retained by your memory. This is your astral being. So while in that instant you have lost your human identity, you have not lost your unique individuality. If you have formulated a precise idea of how you wish to look and feel after you have passed over, then you will find exactly that. You will be just as you expected to be.

And you can change again, whenever you consciously wish it. You can even change continually if you want to.

AND BEYOND

So where do you go from there? Well, you are not submitted to any more fearful judgement than your own – and then only when you are ready to meet it. This comes in the form of a life review and self-assessment. However, your soul (which knows everything about all your deeds) is the harshest judge of all. With the soul there can be no excuses, no swaying the jury or getting off on a clever technicality.

Let's say, for example, you wilfully caused mental or physical suffering to other human beings or to animals during your physical life. Yes, there is payback for your cruelty, but you get to choose in which way it is paid. You might decide to return to the human world, being born into a new body, in order to improve on your last life. You might decide to spend what equates with an eternity in human terms helping those you have hurt or killed and others like them. You might decide to remain as you were in your lifetime, existing with others of the same mental attitude and persuasion, without making any further progress. The choice is yours (though the recycle bin gets an awful lot of use).

How light and colourful your course depends wholly on you. It is all your decision. When you wish to progress by returning to physical life or by entering the afterlife, you call on a watcher, a guide, and make the shift across.

It is in the afterlife that we fully absorb the consequence of our desires and exploits, whatever they were. Imagine for a moment that you have lived numerous lives in various bodies, have died many agonising or traumatic deaths and have killed, raped, looted, destroying the lives and happiness of goodness knows how many others along the way. (Inevitably there will be some nice bits too, but they won't be weighing so heavily in your thoughts in this moment!)

Now imagine that you've just died. In that instant you are amazed, delighted, and then (only a little later) alarmed to find yourself still with thought and the ability to sense everything. At the same moment, you suddenly become super-aware of all your previous misdemeanours resonating deep within you. They flood through you unchecked and leave you sickened and shocked.

Then you notice a being standing quietly nearby. This being gives you a sense of comfort and warmth – good feelings. Suddenly you realise that the being is talking to you through thought waves you can understand and respond to. This being is your guide. He or she explains that they have been with you, watching over you, throughout your life, whether you knew it or not, and that you had both agreed to this beforehand. Gently but firmly you are then asked some significant questions:

- Do you wish to go back into another physical life and put right the misdemeanours you have committed?
- Do you wish to stay here and make amends for all the suffering you have caused?
- Do you wish to learn more while you are here, and go on to join your soul group (a group of like-minded and compatible beings)?

Think of your life today. How many times have you repeated the same mistake? Have you continued to pick the wrong type of partner in relationships? Have you taken any old job just for the money? Have you kept telling yourself, 'I'm not ready – I'll do that tomorrow/next month/next year'? Pretty soon it all becomes monotonously cyclic, and before you know it you're in your nineties, wishing you'd made the change and created the shift when you were younger.

ARE YOU IN REPLAY YET AGAIN?

Now imagine all of this happening to you again and again, over numerous lifetimes. An awful thought, isn't it? But history repeats itself and individuals are no exception. If you have recognised that you are presently living a cyclical life, you are being given this truth now because this is a time when you are able to make the effort to 'go for it' and change. If you don't make this change, you could be repeating the same old lessons in life after life for eternity! Understanding and accepting reincarnation really requires only a small expansion in your consciousness. Under the laws of karma, your actions in one life will affect all of your lives thereafter. Clever words, but put simply this is just cause and effect.

Of course, when you are existing in the afterlife dimension, enjoying all manner of creativity and closely bonding with other like-minded souls, it is hard to leave it and return to another physical life when those living have finished mourning your death and it is time for you to move on.

In the human world, when someone close to you passes away, the feeling of loss can be immense. The closer the bond, the greater the grief, and it is only made worse if the passing was traumatic, sudden or unexpected. We take so much for granted while living. Some people also suffer shock and regret when they pass over, and may even wish to stay close to a loved one, endeavouring to make some form of contact or get a specific message through to them, perhaps something they never said while alive. But this can make it all the more difficult for the one (or ones) still living, as it will prevent them from completing their mourning. Instead, they will continue their mission of sorrow without closure.

The extreme outcome of this inability to let go is the creation of a negative field that encases and traps the soul until finally the living can let go. Only then can peace and progression take place for the soul.

YOUNG AND OLD SOULS

A young soul or an old soul? What is this all about? I firmly believe that every soul chooses when and how to come into life, and indeed the precise physical body that it will inhabit. You might feel that, given the choice, you would seek perfection in the living world, selecting the most attractive body you could conjure up to inhabit, but that is misplaced thinking. The old adage 'beauty is in the eye of the beholder' rings true; real beauty has nothing to do with an in-vogue appearance. While the body may be freely chosen, it must be taken from within the confines of our level of spiritual progress at the time. You move up the levels only slowly as you progress spiritually.

The old soul has been back in the recycle bin many times over; has been there, done that, read all the books and seen every one of the films; and has a vast reservoir of experience to draw upon; so it knows better than to keep repeating the same old mistakes. But the young soul has still to develop from the original cell. It has no knowledge, experience or previous learning already lodged in its memory.

Understandably, a young soul does not generally want to 'go the distance' by taking chances or seeking out great adventures in life. They are far more likely to prefer a steady job and to be careful with money. They may be quite shy, even fearful of upsetting the social system. For a young soul it is enough just being here and to be making their way.

So which one are you? It is healthy to ask this question as soon as you can. The more you experience out there, the more you absorb, and all of it is progress. Spirituality is sought by necessity; it is an aspect of the common need to search for new ideas and attitudes. One of the greatest spiritual acts is giving, out of loving kindness, no more no less. Finding and maintaining your own spiritual integrity comes with an understanding and acceptance of why you are here now, so I beg you to give this question some thought.

You should also give some thought to your thoughts. Thought is normally considered to be hidden, private and personal, but it may not actually be so. Strong thoughts, for example, can be either positive or negative in nature, and will work for or against you, as thought creates an active energy. It is the material embodiment of destructive thought that causes most of the misery and distress in the world, while constructive thought is generally beneficial to the world, unless extreme material limitations hinder the flow.

The one thing everyone seeks is happiness, the degree of which can only be determined by the power and wise use of will in the conscious mind. It is a part of human nature to seek individuality, but eventually we find we are all part of a much greater plan.

GHOST PEOPLE

I use the term 'ghost people' rather than 'ghosts' simply to remind you that ghosts were once of human flesh and blood. In my definition, there are two main differences between ghosts and spirit people. Whereas spirit people are free to travel wherever they want, throughout the many levels and dimensions of existence, ghost people continue to be attached to the physical plane, i.e. to buildings, the land and the living. They are stuck fast in the etched memory of their last life and death, thereby almost certainly causing themselves great and prolonged suffering. They remain engaged with negative thought processes belonging to their past life, and these have become immensely strong and dense.

In the course of my ghost-busting work in the UK and abroad, I have received many communications from ghost people. I have found that they very often seek a potential alternative life force from the living, as if this can be used to replace their own. Since, as I have said, they are bound, literally, to the area they knew while they were alive (and often, too, to the place of their dying, depending on the circumstances), when I am ghost-busting the first thing I do is look for their boundary zone and then walk around it, so that I can make myself known to the ghost person concerned and let them know why I am visiting.

Just imagine for a moment being a ghost, feeling totally lost and alone, and yet not knowing how to shift away and release yourself from all that you have known in your life. Imagine how terrible that must be. Add to that the possibility of a slow, painful or traumatic death, perhaps at the hand of another, and you can understand why a ghost person might feel cheated, or even robbed of their life.

For these reasons, I generally find it best to empathise and reason firmly when working with ghost people. Sometimes, however, their deep-seated rage and aggression can be insurmountable and they will stubbornly (and amazingly viciously) resist all attempts to help them move on. That is when a special force comes in to assist the proceedings, as I have been only too pleased and relieved to find out on several occasions. I jokingly call this force the spirit police, as they have always appeared to me dressed in tight, zipped-up black uniforms and looking very smart indeed! These special beings have kindly assisted me whenever my own powers of persuasion have let me down, 'arresting' and carting several of the most stubborn ghost people away – mostly in situations where the property's living occupants very badly need to regain their health, strength and sanity in order to get their lives back on track.

With ghost people you can never afford to be complacent, as you can never be sure what you're going to have to deal with next.

Ghost-busting in Norway

On this occasion, I was asked by a journalist if I would travel to Norway to help him deal with a case of haunting that he wanted to make the subject of a major article in his magazine. He stipulated that I should know nothing at all about the circumstances of the case (which is the way I like to work anyway), and he wouldn't even tell me where I was going to be taken. Not that I minded this at all, for now it seemed as if I was embarking on a proper mystery adventure.

I was duly met at the airport by the journalist and his photographer. We then drove for hours, only making small-talk – no facts pertinent to the case – eventually arriving at a small town, where I was told we were a few minutes away from the destination.

After relaxing and having a bite to eat, we drove on to a large old two-storey hotel, the three wings of which were built around a central courtyard open at the front. I got out of the car and was walking into the courtyard, moving towards the main entrance, when a ground-floor door at the end of a side wing (in fact, the door nearest to me) suddenly banged wide open. We looked, but there was nobody there. The journalist went very quiet.

I looked again and was aware there was now a ghost person, a man, standing in this same open doorway, watching me. I starting laughing and said, 'Oh, well, at least I'm expected', and with that the door was slammed shut. Very nervously, the journalist laughed at my joke.

I had warned my companions that I have to be left to my own devices when I am working. I explained that they were welcome to follow me but were not to speak at all. I always give my own running commentary as I go along. To me, ghost-busting is like doing a survey; it is my job to give as much specific information on the ghost person or people as I can – names, dates when they died, how they died and, more importantly, why they are trapped, where they are and what upset or damage they've been causing the occupants, such as creating illness, depression, headaches and so on. If you have not yet had an experience of ghost-busting, you would be amazed at what you can find out this way – some ghosts are really quite boastful about what they get up to!

Now it turned out that this hotel was a 'double-decker' – my nickname for a place where there are numerous ghosts spanning hundreds of years – but the particular ghost I wish to talk about here, and the one who touched my heart, was down in the cellar.

He was a young boy, who showed me where he had been left, beaten and starving, to die shackled and chained to the stone floor, some 50 years ago. He then took me to where he had been buried, in a hole that was now covered by a drain cover. He told me his bones had later been moved and pointed out the place where they now were. He gave me, in his own words, his name, the dates of his birth and death and the name of the person who had murdered him.

So I did my work with humility and love, and helped him to move on to a freedom he could never have imagined existed up until then, in a place where he could at last enjoy each and every one of the wonders of existence.

The hotel owners had also been following me as I moved around, saying nothing but listening intently to all the details I reported, and by now they had become very upset and emotional.

Later, over a drink, they admitted that when the hotel was refurbished they had removed the remains of what looked like shackles fixed into the cellar flags, as well as the buried bones of a child all exactly where I had said they were, adding that they had then reburied the child's remains in the place I had pointed out in the garden. It was all just as this poor little boy had told me! Now, fortunately, he is free, safe and happy.

DESTINY

Destiny to me is like a disc that was recorded earlier. Individual discs exist for every person and each creature living. Each country (as well as other geographical zones) also has its own recording, on a layered world disc. Throughout the history of our civilisation, the majority of people have had a block about that knowledge – a block due to an in-built and unconscious fear and the desire for self-preservation. It is so much easier to live life in denial of such things. But, thankfully, there has always been a small minority whose consciousness is more expansive, while today a growing number of people are healthily questioning and wishing to know.

I can only give a sad smile when I think about the bitterness and turmoil that exists on our planet, with its myriad wars breeding and feeding hatred on a global scale. Every time the outcome gives us a harsher lesson, yet the sum total goes on increasing and will continue to increase until mankind – individually and as a whole – is ready to hear and listens. The Earth's clock is ticking. Endeavouring to make the effort to know more beyond the now is an absolute written necessity for our survival. We are not alone.

Conclusion

This unique book is my way of sharing with you the spiritual journey. I trust that it will give you the key to activate your own psychic powers. I wish you well in this work of unlocking, and in all your psychic adventures to come.

Your voyage of exploration into other realms has now properly begun. These will provide you with amazing opportunities for self-empowerment and spiritual development, helping you to create an ever stronger union with your soul or higher self.

Now that you have found the courage to experiment and have mastered the techniques employed in this book, I guarantee that they will serve you well throughout the rest of your life. If you can at least embrace the positive changes and harness your innate ability to handle the transitions involved, then you will very greatly enhance your ability to achieve what you truly set out to do and which was, perhaps, quite beyond your wildest dreams only a short while ago. And if you can then share this understanding and learning with just one other person, then you are assisting the expansion of a world consciousness that makes your journey all the more worthwhile.

To me, it is interesting to compare the way that humankind thought before the last World War with the way it thinks now. Then, belief systems were much simpler – total faith in religion, in the status and reputation of the nation, in the government and in the armed forces, together with an overriding acceptance of duty and discipline. But in the aftermath of that War the baby-boomer generation was born (between the late 1940s and early 1960s), of which I am a member. With this generation a whole new belief system came too. A greater freedom of expression suddenly began to emerge, egged on by the failure of the Vietnam War, the assassinations of the Kennedy brothers and Martin Luther King and the peaceful rebellion of the hippies during the flower power period of the mid-sixties. All of which quickly eroded old values.

The sacred idols that had been worshipped before – religion, state, the military, the unwritten code of duty – all suddenly became tarnished and old hat. Now, in the Western world at least, we live in an age of the endless empty promotion of individual celebrity, rampant consumerism and reduced personal responsibility, a time in which the demands and expectations of instant gratification seem only to increase as we remain cocooned in an false sense of credit-card security. But none of this contributes anything that is remotely valuable to the nourishment of the soul, let alone beneficial in the true service of helping each other to live and flourish together as human beings.

We all make 'mistakes'. In my view, however, there are no true mistakes. A mistake is simply a way of learning, and if not understood or learnt the first time it will be called in again.

Despite the threats of extremism (of whatever belief) I sense that there is a gradual, ever-increasing spiritual enlightenment sweeping around the globe, as a growing number of lost and rudderless human beings begin to turn away from the current false gods of material wealth and vicarious excitement, and instead attempt to rediscover true spirituality, and with it a sense of community and the common good. So start seeking to understand the deeper meaning of your small everyday encounters. Use your new talents to see truly useful ways of assisting others. As a psychic, you can and will be a beacon to others, lighting their way through periods of adversity and stress, as well as giving them moments of happiness and inspiration.

Having walked your talk and drawn your deepest wishes towards you, now develop your psychic powers to go forward positively. Give thought when you wake up in the morning and see a perfect, sunny day – whatever the weather is like outside. Remember that positivity and optimism will enhance, energise and brighten your 'field' – and will influence all those around you. That power can be truly immense.

I feel truly excited to be here. I hope you do too. Give gratitude in your thoughts that here you are, and acknowledge all those who help to make your days worthwhile. And don't forget to help others in return. Remember to be constantly aware of our wonderful planet's beauty, as well as of the fact that we, like all of life, rely upon it.

 PSYCHIC TAKEAWAY: **THE GREATEST TAKEAWAY FOR YOUR LIFE**

Finally, here is one last psychic takeaway for you. Use it to make your wish.

- Plan your moment, sit in a quiet spot, take three breaths in and out, and close your eyes.
- Now put your wish in words in the following way:
  I wish to have . . . . . . in my life now, in the most divine way.
- Visualise the words in a balloon and let it float up into the sky.
- Take a breath, open your eyes and let it be. Now go and do something else. But remember, from this moment on:
  FEEL IT,
  ACT IT,
  KNOW IT AND WALK IT IN THE NOW (as though you already have it).
  You must maintain that feeling and that power through positive energy – which equals enthusiasm and true passion.

I have written the following to assist you in bringing about your own self-empowered state. Read it first thing in the morning or last thing at night for a couple of weeks, and then whenever you feel you need a boost. It is magical – as you will find out.

> In the moment of now
> I am the power, I am the light, I am all I wish.
> I now call upon the power from the universe
> To pour into me from this moment on.
> It heals me, it energises me, it makes me smile with delight.
> I now have all I wished to be in and around me.
> I now have the people and the enjoyment of my life's work
> Before me, to share with all, exuding a glow of positive
> Light, pulsating over the airwaves, giving a positive field of
> Love across the world, radiated from our universe.

With my love, thoughts and smiles,

Angela Donovan

Glossary

Adept A person who is spiritually attuned and a skilled initiate in psychic work.

Astral The subtle soul body attached to the physical body.

Beyond A dimension outside the physical.

Code A Brain wave frequency (presently) at 7.83 hertz.

Clairaudience Hearing by extra-sensory means.

Clairsentience Picking up and translating energy fields by sensing.

Clairvoyance Seeing visions by extra-sensory means.

Energy force Strong positive or negative fields of energy that can be felt.

Entities Beings that once lived and now exist as forms of strong negative energy.

Etheric body The important 'shell' around the physical body that absorbs vitality.

Ghost people People who have died but still exist amongst the living unable to free themselves from their negative memories.

Laws of the universe The means by which the Highest Intelligence maintains order, harmony and balance throughout the universe.

Memory disc Memories that usually lie dormant within the human mind but can be accessed.

Medium A trained go-between who acts as intermediary between the physical and other dimensions.

Passed over The moment of death and leaving of the physical body.

Previous life Any life lived before the current one.

Psychic A sensitive person with the ability to use their subtle senses to receive and translate information from other dimensions than the physical.

Psychic rules Rules laid out to assist the working progress of a psychic.

Shaman An initiate originating from Siberian tribes who can work in Code A through ritual work.

Spirit The embodiment of the soul in the afterlife.

Spirit guide One who has chosen to work with living individuals as well as those needing guidance in the afterlife.

Spirit net The source. An immensely powerful zone linked to the universe, where all information is held. Records exist on all who have ever lived in the world, marking every deed and event that has ever taken place. Includes all other life forms.

Spirit teachers Spirit people who can communicate their teaching to those of the living who are spiritually attuned to learn.

Spiritual integrity Adherence to honest principles with a divine purpose.

Stage The place you have reached in your spiritual progress.

Third eye A faculty that can be activated in the mind giving the ability to see beyond physical boundaries of sight and time.

True will The ability to act or refrain from acting at any one time.

Tuning disc A part of the brain that can be psychically tuned and activated.

Tuning in/out The training of the brain to go on and off a specific brain wave on command, i.e. 7.83 hertz.

Universal laws Rules made by universal leaders affecting all who live or exist in the world.

Written path The path of life already laid down.

Resources

Healing

National Federation of Spiritual Healers (NFSH)
Old Manor Farm Studios
Church Street
Sunbury-on-Thames
Middlesex TW16 6RG

Tel: (0)1932 783164
Web: www.nfsh.org.uk

Founded over 50 years ago. Has offices across the globe.

Spiritualism

Spiritualist Association of Great Britain (SAGB)
33 Belgrave Square
London SW1X 8QB

Tel: (0)20 7235 3351
Web: www.sagb.org.uk

Training in mediumship

The College of Psychic Studies
16 Queensbury Place
London SW7 2EB

Tel: (0)20 7589 3292
Web: www.collegeofpsychicstudies.co.uk

Psychic and spiritual magazines and newspapers

Chat – It's Fate
IPC Connect Ltd
King's Reach Tower
Stamford Street
London SE1 9LS
Tel: 0870 444 5000

Fate & Fortune
H Bauer Publishing
Academic House
24-28 Oval Road
London NW1 7DT
Tel: (0)20 7241 8000
Email: www.fate.fortune@
bauer.co.uk

Kindred Spirit
Sandwell Barns
Haberton
Totnes
Devon TQ9 7LJ
Tel: (0)1803 866 686

The Psychic News
Psychic Press 1995 Ltd
The Coach House
Stansted Hall
Stansted
Essex CM24 8UD
Tel: (0)1279 817050
Web: www.thepsychicnews
bookshop.co.uk

Spirit & Destiny
H Bauer Publishing
Academic House
24-28 Oval Road
London NW1 7DT
Tel: (0)20 7241 8000
Email: www.spirit.destiny@
bauer.co.uk

Index